Croagh Patrick and the Islands of Clew Bay

A Guide to the Edge of Europe

Michael Cusack

ISBN-13: 978-1530378463
ISBN-10: 153037846X

First Edition: April 2016

Printed in Westport, Ireland by Berry Print Group

Contents

Foreword

I was born ninety-seven years ago in Rosbeg, in 1919. This pretty village lies on an inlet of Clew Bay where the land slopes into the sea, not far from Croagh Patrick, and from where some of the myriad islands described in this book may be seen.

Walter Macken said if you want to know the beginning of any story, you would have to go back to Adam. I can't do that, but with the help of my family, I can go back to the 19th century when Westport became a port.

It all started with shoals of herring finding their way inside Clare Island and, eventually, right into Inishlyre with its natural harbour. This was good news for Westport and for maritime Europe. Unfortunately, the shoals of herring were not always such good news for local boatman. In 1886, two of my uncles were persuaded to take barrel loads of the fish from Clare Island. So heavy was the load it broke the back of their new 26-ton cutter 'Spirit' and she sank off Carrowmore Point.

My paternal grandfather died before I was born, but as Admiralty Pilot for the west coast of Ireland he knew all the islands and left his stories for us to enjoy. Fortunately, as one of the last of the Westport pilots, my father Peter Hopkins kept us in touch with heavenly Clew Bay and its memorable inhabitants. My father had every reason to remember the hospitality of the islanders – when it was too stormy for him to return to Westport, he was readily made welcome to stay the night on whichever island he happened to be near at the time. We were especially grateful to learn from him that my grandfather would drop bags of meal into the occupied in-shore islands during the famine.

It was always a pleasure for us children to visit islands where we had friends. I will remember forever the three families of Gibbons's on Inishlyre. May was the school teacher on Cullen, or Collan More as it is known today. Then there were the Kelly's of Islandmore who, tragically, lost their youngest son, Paddy, one night at Westport Quay. I believe he fell from the ship's gangway.

I won't forget the Higgins's on Inisheeny, nor Paddy Joyce who had a light shining always on Inishraher….

Foreword

Almost all the islands are uninhabited now, but we who are left will remember other days and other ways, the left-over echoes of people who came and went and always left something of themselves behind. We'll remember other music makers. Maybe we'll hear the lilt of an islander's voice on the wind. We won't forget those we knew in the buried past.

I hope that you enjoy reading this book as much as I have. It brings to light many little-known facts about the islands that will be revealing even to those who have lived in this wonderful area all of their lives.

Gerardine Cusack
Author of 'A Nightingale Sang'
March 17th 2016

Preface

Croagh Patrick and the islands of Clew Bay are an inspiration for thousands of visitors each year to this remote area on the western edge of Europe. According to popular legend there are 365 islands in Clew Bay – one for each day of the year. There are far more than a few unnamed 'islands', 'islets' and clusters of rocks in the bay, particularly south of Illanataggart and in the area of Forillan and Stony Islands (which lie just northeast and east of Inishgowla South Island, in Westport Bay). There are also dozens of 'drowned' drumlins lying just beneath the waters of the bay. Whether these, together with the named islands and rocks listed here, make up the fabled number is a matter for argument amongst those better informed.

For the purposes of this book, the word 'Island' is defined as any tract of sub-continental land surrounded by water – even in the presence of a land bridge - that remains visible in benign conditions when the tide reaches its high water mark.

This book is intended to give the reader access to information to the Clew Bay islands and Croagh Patrick that previously would have required a great deal of time and effort to uncover. The information regarding the Reek is not intended to emulate the many excellent brochures and other information regarding its storied past, but rather to outline details that may not be obvious from the outset. Conversely, remarkably little has ever been written about the islands of Clew Bay, other than their relationship to the ice age.

In summary, this is the outcome of significant research, both field and academic, and attempts to represent known facts about Croagh Patrick and the islands of the Clew Bay. As with any project of this scale, there is margin for error, and the author welcomes any input that would further enhance the accuracy of this research. He can be reached via email at olcc@att.net.

Introduction

The Irish name for Clew Bay is Cuan Mó or Cuan Modha. Where the name 'Clew' came from is a source of conjecture. Modha appears to have been derived from the name of a Pagan chieftain.

Some say that the tribe known as the Tuatha-de-Danaan came to Clew Bay in long ships propelled by galley slaves and Irish prisoners, and overthrew the resident Fir Bolgs. The tribal king Manannan (who gave his name to the Isle of Man) was said to have hunted wild boar in the woods around Croagh Patrick. The Tuatha-de-Danaan were followed by the final race to settle in Ireland, the Milesians.

Knox, in his 'History of County Mayo', notes that "old chroniclers allege, that years after the Milesians came to Ireland, there were fierce battles fought about Cruáchan Aigle (now Croagh Patrick), Cleire (Clare Island) and Inisheemow (the other islands of Clew Bay), and that the chief races of ancient Ireland were brought together at Murrisk – De Danaans, Firbolgs and Milesians inter-married and produced a new race, the tribes as such being actually submerged."

The islands of Clew Bay – excluding the mighty guardian of Clare Island - lie more or less between Croagh Patrick to the south and the Nephin Mountains to the north. Croagh Patrick is considered a holy mountain to Christians and has a chapel on the summit. It is called 'The Reek' locally. The Nephins are a remote range of hills stretching towards north Mayo, and include the solitary Nephin mountain, which is the second highest peak in the province of Connaught, after Mweelrea.

Croagh Patrick and Clare Island are the two most recognizable icons in the Clew Bay area. It is also believed by many that there is an island for every day of the year in the bay – or a total of 365. Much depends upon the definition of 'island', but even at high tide there are arguably more than one hundred named pieces of land – mostly drumlins – and rock outcrops surrounded by water within the confines of the bay. Drumlins are the remnants of lateral moraines left behind by the last ice age, boulder clay and gravel covered with soil and grass. As a result of sonar surveys in the bay, there are known to be twice as many rock outcrops and drowned drumlins beneath the Atlantic waves.

Introduction

Clew Bay is a wide, Atlantic Ocean-facing bay. Its drumlin landscape was formed during the last glacial period. The sea subsequently flooded this area, creating dozens of islands between interlocking bays. The bay is also believed to have the most significant shingle reserves in the country, and has (on the islands) the only examples of incipient gravel barriers in Ireland.

Evidence of early colonisation around Clew Bay is evidenced by many archaeological remains, such as those in the vicinity of Kildangan and the standing stone near Annagh Head in Murrisk, which is said to mark the graves of Pagan chiefs.

When William Thackeray, the English novelist, visited the area a few years before the great famine, he wrote of Clew Bay that it was "the most beautiful view I ever saw in the world…the bay and the Reek, which sweeps down to the sea, and the hundred isles in it, were dressed up in gold and purple and crimson, with the whole cloudy west in a flame. Wonderful, wonderful!"

There are strong tidal races around the outer islands of the bay, particularly at the Inishgort lighthouse, and also around the gaps between Bartraw, Inishdaugh and Dorinish. Tidal flows are also strong in the Newport Channel.

Several of the islands of Clew Bay are tidal. Sea levels can rise over ten feet in the bay on a typical day. Several of the 'outer' islands of Westport Bay are also connected to each other at low tide. It is not unusual to see 'roads' across the tidal flats that are used by farmers to get supplies and livestock to and from these seemingly remote places. Although there are now only five or six islands inhabited year round, prior to the famine years the majority of islands larger than a few acres had many occupants.

Most of the large outer islands are inaccessible other than by boat, while those in the shallower waters of Westport and Newport Bays may be reached by other means. Of course, these include islands that have been connected to the mainland by a causeway or bridge, such as Rosmore, Inishnakillew and Inishcottle, but even islands that looking at a map may appear to be far out in the bay.

One such island is Collan More, which is the largest mass of offshore land in the area, apart from Clare Island. Collan More (Collainn Mhór –

Introduction

formerly Cuileann or Holly Island) is a large inhabited island situated in Newport Bay, just northwest of Rosmoney Pier. It can also be seen from the mainland at Roscahill, about nine kilometres from Westport (left off the N59 after about five kilometres and about three kilometres west).

Collan More is a long island, stretching from west to east. At its westernmost end is the island of Collan Beg. The island was inhabited by 218 people in 1841. In 1911, it included Collanmore National School and nine private dwellings occupied by forty people. By 2006, there were just eighteen inhabitants and the school had closed.

A stone's throw away is the island of Inishgort, home of the only working lighthouse in the area, and the entrance to Westport Bay.

South of Collan More, on the other side of Rosmoney, are two other islands. Crovinish (Croibhinis – formerly Creamh Inis or Garlic Island) is an uninhabited island, southeast of Inishlyre and northwest of Inishgowla South. In 1841, the island had twenty-two inhabitants, and by 1911 there were still sixteen people living on the island in three thatched dwellings, each of which had two rooms. Sixty-year-old Martin Fadden and his thirty-nine-year-old wife Mary lived in one home with their eight children at that time.

Illanataggart (Oileán an tSagairt – Priest's Island) is also currently uninhabited. In 1841, however, there were 33 persons living on this island and by 1911 just seven resided there.

Beyond Clynish are the islands of Inishnakillew (Inis na Coille or 'island of the wood'), Inishcottle (Inish Coitil or 'Cottle's Island') and Moneybeg. Inishnakillew is connected to the mainland by a causeway, and the more remote Inishcottle is connected to Inishnakillew by another causeway. Both of these islands are currently inhabited. An area known as Carrigeenglass to the south of Inishcottle borders Moneybeg Island. Here, a channel divides the island from the bigger mass of Clynish, which is one of the islands in Clew Bay currently inhabited. In 1841 there were 87 people living on Clynish. In 1911, twenty-three people lived in three dwellings. By 2006, there were just five inhabitants.

North of Collan More, the coastline of Newport Bay is deeply indented. Here there are long, narrow peninsulas of land that in several cases are barely connected to the mainland by bridges or causeways. Although several of these fractured pieces of land are not specifically identified as 'islands', they retain a tenuous relationship with the mainland.

Attached to one of the peninsulas is Rosmore. This 'island' is divided from the mainland by a 20-foot wide channel, which is crossed by a bridge.

There are other 'mainland islands' along the shores of Newport Bay, including Rosbarnagh (to the right of Rossanrubble peninsula), Inishturlin (northwest of Rosbarnagh), Roslaher/Rosbeg (south of Rossanrubble), Roslynagh (north of Inishdaweel), and Rosturk (north, towards Mulranny).

There are a number of islands near the town of Westport, including Annagh (Oileán an Eanaigh), which is an uninhabited group of three islands situated in Westport Bay, just east of Murrisk. The islands are named Annagh West, Annagh Middle and Annagh East. These are located just off the Murrisk road, about nine kilometres from Westport. In 1841, Annagh East was inhabited by 33 people. Little trace of any dwelling remains today. Another is Cahernaran Island (Oileán Chathair na Reann), which is an uninhabited island situated in Westport Bay, south of Inisheeny. It is located just off the R335 road towards Louisburgh, on the right just before the Great Famine monument in Murrisk, about nine kilometres west of Westport (right at Carrowsallagh). Cahernaran is known for an ancient stone fort, now destroyed. Illanroe (Red Island) is close to Rosbeg, about three kilometres out of town.

There is no naturally occurring potable water on any of the uninhabited islands of Clew Bay. All of the inhabited islands had been given piers and/or pontoons, and most have mains water and electricity. Many of the islands are interconnected by shingle bars, particularly at lower tides. Islandmore, Rabbit Island, Derrinish and Inishbee are good examples of this.

There are some derelict farms on the uninhabited islands, which are a more recent testament to the high population that once inhabited the bay. There are also many of the inappropriately named lazybeds – or potato growing activity prior to the famine years.

Croagh Patrick and the Islands

Croagh Patrick, known locally as 'The Reek', is a 765-metre (2,510 feet) high mountain that dominates the landscape around the picturesque town of Westport. Once a place of pagan worship, today it is considered Ireland's holiest mountain because of its association with Saint Patrick, who in the fifth century is believed to have spent forty days and nights fasting on its summit. There are many stories and legends associated with this beautiful peak.

On the last Sunday in July, a day known as 'Reek Sunday', thousands of pilgrims ascend the mountain. The normal pilgrimage route today is via the village of Murrisk, which is located about ten kilometres west of Westport. There are other ancient routes up the mountain, including the Tóchar Phádraig, which approaches from the eastern side, the Lecanvey Route from the west, and the Owenwee from the south.

On a clear day, the views from Croagh Patrick are stunning, both to the north, where the islands of Clew Bay and Nephin Mountains provide a backdrop that rivals any on the planet, and to the south, where the mountain ranges of Partry, Sheeffry, and Mweelrea give way to the Maumturks and Twelve Bens of Connemara.

Croagh Patrick, or Cruáchan Aigle, as it used to be known, has drawn pilgrims for thousands of years. Archaeologists are still uncovering long forgotten artifacts and other associations with the mountain, such as the 'rolling sun' phenomenon as seen twice a year (on April 18th and August 24th) from the Boheh Stone near Westport, which also exhibits Neolithic rock art. The standing stones at Killadangan (on the right just before Murrisk when travelling from Westport) align with the sun on the winter solstice. The Clew Bay Archaeological Trail explores six thousand years of such history in the area.

Excavations on the top of Croagh Patrick determined that it had once functioned as a hill fort, with several dwellings on the summit. Local archaeologist Gerry Walsh's team also discovered the outlines of at least thirty hut sites. Further excavations also uncovered the foundations of an early church, dating as far back as the fifth century, when Saint Patrick was alive.

The mountain has attracted many interesting individuals, including 'Bob of the Reek' – a pilgrim who is said to have spent fourteen years on the mountain in the early twentieth century, living on the north face much of the year, but spending winters with a Murrisk family. Bob climbed to the top of Croagh Patrick every day. His 'cave', which still survives, was most likely a holy well from medieval times. In accordance with his wishes, he was buried on the top of the mountain, near the chapel that was built in 1905.

A short walk to the statue of Saint Patrick on the Reek often reveals stunning views of Clew Bay and the distant Nephin mountains, but (apart from the massive Clare Island to the west) how can you tell one island from another? Here are some clues:

- The semi-island at the end of the long strip of land reaching from the shore out into the bay is called Bartraw. It is one of the most popular destinations in the area

- The island just off the tip of Bartraw is called Inishdaugh. Legend has it that Danish treasure is buried there

- To the left of Inishdaugh is Inishleague, behind which are Inishimmel and Inishlaghan, while to its right is the island of Inisheeny, now uninhabited but once home to several families

- The connected islands that look like a prehistoric bird with a long tail (furthest west from Bartraw) are Dorinish Beg and Dorinish More, once owned by Beatle John Lennon and once home to a commune of hippies led by Sid Rawle
- The large island inside Westport Bay with a prominent white house at its eastern tip is Inishraher, now a Transcendental Meditation (TM) retreat

- The tiny island to the east of Inishraher is called Corillan or 'The Scotsman's Bonnet'

- The island at the end of the Murrisk peninsula (closest to the Reek and just beyond Murrisk Abbey) is called Cahernaran, and once had its own fort

- Beyond Cahernaran, further down the coast towards Westport, are the three islands of Annagh – East, Middle and West joined by narrow strips of land and shingle - now empty but once home to over thirty people

- The island that boasts the only working lighthouse in Clew Bay (the white structure visible just beyond the 'tail' of Dorinish) is called Inishgort

- The island with a cluster of buildings to the southeast of Inishgort is Inishlyre, whose deep natural harbour used to be used as a dropping off point by larger ships with cargo for Westport Quay. A family still lives on the island

- The large islands behind Inishgort are Island More and Knockycahillaun, which once housed several families and are part of a network of islands connected by shingle bars. A new holiday home and the old houses are visible where the two islands meet

- Beyond the Island More chain, the distant shingle bar jutting straight out into the bay is part of Inishbee island, beyond which lies the beautiful island of Inishoo

- Further north and east of Inishoo are the myriad islands of Newport Bay and the Nephin Mountains, one of the wildest and most remote areas in the entire country

- Looking further west from the Nephins is the Corraun Peninsula, and beyond that is the island of Achillbeg and Achill Island itself, the largest offshore island in Ireland, with its cliffs of Croaghaun - the third highest sea cliffs in Europe

- It is not unusual to see rain sweeping over the Nephin Mountains, while the Reek may be bathed in sunshine, and vice-versa. When the wind swings to the northwest, the impressive form of Clare Island being suddenly obliterated by mist is often a harbinger of a squall heading for Croagh Patrick.

Tóchar Phádraig – The Original Pilgrimage Path

Tóchar Phádraig, or Patrick's Causeway, is an ancient pilgrimage route that today begins at the 13th century Ballintubber Abbey and finishes some thirty kilometres away, on Croagh Patrick. While some would argue that the true pilgrimage route begins at Aughagower, from where Saint Patrick is said to have walked to the Reek to begin his fast, the Croagh Patrick Heritage Trail have extended it beyond Ballintubber to Mayo Abbey near the town of Balla.

In pagan times, it was part of a route from Rathcroghan in County Roscommon, formerly the seat of the high kings of Connaught, to what was then known as Cruáchan Aigle, which some attest was the pagan name for the Reek called after Aigle, who in mythology killed Ciara, daughter of Lugh (after whom the festival of Lughnasa is named). Other historians believe that Croagh Patrick was named Cruáchan Aigli, meaning 'eagle'. The pilgrimage to Croagh Patrick takes place on the Sunday before the festival of Lughnasa, in other words, the last Sunday in July. The Tóchar is known as a 'causeway' because it was originally built to carry heavy traffic, such as horse-drawn 'chariots', across the boggy terrain.

During penal times (when a series of laws were imposed in an attempt to force Irish Roman Catholics and Protestant dissenters to accept a reformed denomination as defined by the Anglican Church), a man who became known as Sean na Sagart was employed to hunt priests in the area. Despite the best efforts of the locals to protect the priests, this man enjoyed some success before he himself was stabbed to death. The trail passed close to a lake known as Lough na gCeann – Lake of the Heads – where it is said that Sean disposed of his victims' heads after claiming his reward.

The trail follows the mysterious Aille River for about a mile before it disappears underground. The Aille is the site of what is called the 'Tuille Sidhe' or Fairy Tide, when it floods. It was here that 160 people in the service of Aedh ua Conchobair, a former King of Connaught, were said to have died when their enemies blocked off the entrance to the caves where the Aille vanishes deep beneath the ground.

Crossing several of over one hundred stiles that Ballintubber Abbey have established along the way, the pilgrim then comes to a place named Teampleshaunaglasha which contains the ruins of a church that was abandoned in 1562. It is believed that the 'Shaun' in the name was a hermit who lived in this place in later years. The ruins were surrounded by a Killeen – an unbaptized infants' graveyard – and other graves from the famine years. There are several legends associated with this place, particularly those involving the terrible fate of individuals who removed stones or artifacts from the old church.

A bohreen (little road) at Stile 46 leads through overhanging trees to the remains of a famine village that once housed 26 families. A legend tells of a mysterious woman who visited at night to leave food for the starving inhabitants.

Large slabs of limestone are visible as the Aille River emerges from its underground course at Stile 50. Potholers have measured the underground course of the river at Pollflanagan to a depth of 112 feet, where they reported the existence of fish with no eyes. Nearby is another cave known as Pollhondra, where a man named Hondra is said to have hidden after he killed his wife. It seems that there is a tragic story at every turn of this route.

At Stile 57, a depression in the ground reveals a place once called 'The Well of Stringle'. It is here that St. Patrick is said to have baptized many locals when he camped there over two Sundays.

The trail then crosses a hillock known locally as 'Creggaun 'a Damhsa', or the Hillock of the Dancing, where some believe fairies abide. this is followed by another bohreen ('bothareen' or small road) which leads to the impressive cliffs that tower above the River Aille as it vanishes into the earth.

At the village of Coill an Bhaile, the trail turns towards the ancient site of Aughagower ("The field of springs"), which Saint Patrick established as a diocese around 441 a.d. At this turn, the ruined castle of MacPhilbin, who captured one of the O'Rourkes and paid a heavy price in return, dominates the landscape for miles to the west. On the way to Aughagower, the trail crosses a large swath of uncultivated land.

Apart from its impressive round tower, graveyards and churches, Aughagower boasts several artifacts dating back to Saint Patrick's time, including 'Dabhach Phadraig' (Patrick's Vat), 'Tobair na nDeachan' (The Well of the Deacons), and 'Leaba Phadraig' (Patrick's Bed).

Beyond Aughagower the trail passes through Lankill, beyond the extraordinary Rock of Boheh, and heads towards Brackloon Wood with its many stories of caves, hidden treasure and ancient monuments. Now the trail reaches the plain that hosts the Owenwee River (the yellow river) which winds its way around the mountain.

This area used to be covered in oak forest, and the Tóchar followed what is now the 'Deer Wall' up to an elevation of four hundred metres, where old maps name rocks such as 'Leac do Phaidir' (Prayer Stone), before joining 'Casan Padraig' to the top of the mountain.

Gold Mining on the Reek

In the 1980s, a seam of gold was discovered on Croagh Patrick in at least twelve quartz veins, which were estimated could produce 770,000 short tons of ore — potentially over 300,000 troy ounces of gold.

In 1989 plans to mine for gold on Croagh Patrick drew huge opposition from the local community in Mayo, who launched a campaign to protect the mountain from mining. British environmentalist David Bellamy spoke at a rally in Westport at the time. Bellamy said Ireland was "the greenest country in the world", but lagging behind the rest of Europe on environmental issues and that he hoped Croagh Patrick would be a turning point. If Croagh Patrick and its magnificent scenic hinterland was in any other country, he said, it would undoubtedly have been designated a world heritage site. He described as "rank vandalism" the politicians' passive stance in allowing the area to be "put up for grabs" for prospecting licences. Even if the company did extract the gold with the least amount of damage, he said, the ecological and environmental cost would be intolerable.

Paddy Hopkins, Chairman of the Mayo Environmental Group and its secretary Seán O'Malley were determined to protect Croagh Patrick and its environment for future generations. It was widely believed that the rush to extract gold - a process that used cyanide - would gravely threaten the sacred mountain and also undermine farming, fishing and tourism, western Ireland's economic pillars.

Apart from the perceived threat to the country's primary pilgrimage mountain, and its reputation as one of the most striking places in Europe, it was believed that cyanide runoff could poison the crystalline waterways of Mayo and Galway counties and kill the foxes, ferrets, badgers, rabbits, fish, seals and hundreds of species of birds that lived in one of Europe's last remaining areas of blanket bogland.

At the time, as many as nineteen prospecting companies were looking at sites from Croagh Patrick to the valley of Doolough and even the island of Inishturk. Many believed that the area around Croagh Patrick should be designated as a national heritage site, while Doolough should be made a national park.

While neither of these initiatives have resulted in long-term State protection of the mountain or designation of a national park in southwest Mayo, the campaigners would eventually succeed in preventing gold-mining. Mayo County Council elected not to allow mining, deciding that the gold was "fine where it was".

No attempts have been made to mine the mountain since, although the government stance was somewhat ambiguous. According to the Department of Energy: "The government is committed to the active investigation of the country's mineral potential and the development of commercial ore . . . subject to environmental safeguards, as an important source of economic growth and employment opportunity."

There is still a mining path and several remnants of the gold mining prospectors high on the Lecanvey side of the Reek, over twenty-five years after they were forced to abandon the project.

The Pirate Queen

Grace O'Malley, otherwise known as Granuaile or Grania Uaile (phonetically "Grawn-you-ale"), lived from around 1530 to 1603. She was born into the clan Ó Máille (O'Malley), who were said to be descendants of the eldest son of a former high king of Ireland. The clan were the hereditary lords of a territory which included the baronies of Murrisk* to the south of Clew Bay and Burrishoole to the north, which originally included the island of Achill.

The earliest written reference to the O'Malley territory around Murrisk is in the fifth century, when Saint Patrick climbed the mountain then known as Cruachan Aigle, before it was renamed Croagh Patrick. The O'Malleys built Murrisk Abbey for the Augustinian friars in 1457.

According to Hubert Thomas Knox in 'The History of County Mayo', even before Granuaile's time, Clew Bay was a famous resort for smugglers who did an extensive trade with the continent. Clare Island of old is often described as a 'pirate's lair' and the 'Mecca of Smugglers'.

The O'Malleys differed from most of the Irish clans in that they were a true seafaring family. According to the 'Book of Rights' (Leabhar ne gCeart), the O'Malleys paid the King of Connaught, who resided in Cruachan (now known as Rathcroghan near Tulsk in County Roscommon) handsomely for the right to make a living from the seas around Clew Bay and beyond.

The O'Malleys did not engage in fishing alone. Piracy became a hallmark of the clan, particularly during Granuaile's time. The sixteenth century saw the old Gaelic world face an onslaught on land from its powerful neighbour. Granuaile built strongholds around the shores of Clew Bay that only skilled local navigators could negotiate by sea, especially as cartographers only began to map the remote and dangerous channels of the west coast after her reign.

Granuaile spend her childhood at the clan residences at Belclare (between Westport and Murrisk) and Clare Island (the tower which still stands today). She was first married at the age of sixteen to Donal O'Flaherty, whose family ruled what is now more or less the boundaries of Connemara in County Galway. During this time, she bore two children, but also began to take an interest in seafaring activities around the Galway City area, where she and her men are said to have exacted tolls or exchange of cargo for safe passage into the busy port before disappearing into the myriad of inlets around the Connemara coast.

It was highly unusual for a woman to command any position of authority in matters of merchanting, much less piracy. In can only be surmised that Granuaile led by example, and was capable of enduring the hardships known to exist on the brutal Atlantic seaboard around the west coast of Ireland.

Around this time, Elizabeth I began her reign as Queen of England. Using a divide and conquer strategy with the Irish lords, she began to disrupt the power base that had long remained undisturbed west of the Shannon River. Granuaile's husband, whose authority had been diminished, died during this period. However, she successfully defended his island fortress in Lough Corrib against the Joyces, a predominant Galway family.

The O'Flaherty clan would not tolerate a woman as heir to Donal's title and she looked again to the sea as a means of establishing power. She returned to Clew Bay and the tower castle at Clare Island. From here, she had a commanding view of the entire bay, and no ship could pass without being spotted.

Now in her twenties, Grace used her O'Malley influence to establish a fighting force of two hundred men, including the infamous 'Gallowglass' or mercenaries from Scotland. Stories of her exploits spread across the Irish Sea around the time the English queen employed a new strategy of colonisation that was to change the power base in Ireland yet again. Life became a matter of survival against the odds for Granuaile.

Granuaile was in her thirties when she married Richard Bourke. It is believed that her main goal was to acquire Rockfleet (also known as Carrickhowley) Castle and the deeper waters around Burrishoole on the north side of Clew Bay. Here, legend has it that the hawser of her favourite galley was attached to her bedpost at night (which is quite possible when one sees the location of the castle on the shore).

In 1584, Sir Richard Bingham was appointed governor of Connaught province. He believed that the Irish were 'never tamed with words, but with swords'. His brutal tactics were not unlike those of his predecessors.

He captured Granuaile's sons Tiobóid na Long (Tibbot of the Ships) and Murrough O'Flaherty, and her half-brother, Dónal na Píopa. Granuaile petitioned the queen for their release and was invited to meet her at Greenwich Palace.

Granuaile was a native Irish language speaker. She was not known to have spoken English at all. However, it is also believed that she had been educated in Latin and that language was spoken at her meeting with Queen Elizabeth.

Following the meeting, Bingham was temporarily removed from his post as governor, but many of Granuaile's other requests were not met, despite her assurances that she would stop supporting the Irish lords' rebellion. Shortly afterwards, Bingham was restored to his position and Granuaile gave up on the notion that her meeting with the queen had a useful outcome.

Granuaile is believed to have died at Rockfleet Castle in 1603, the same year as Queen Elizabeth. She may have been buried in the ruins of the Cistercian Abbey on Clare Island.

The Wrecks of Clew Bay

Clew Bay is the watery home of many shipwrecks. *Irish Wrecks Online* lists 43 in the vicinity, twenty-two of which are in Westport Bay alone.

In 1588, during Granuaile's lifetime, two ships of the Spanish Armada, the *San Nicolas Prodaneli* and the 1,126 ton *El Gran Grin* – the latter being one of the largest ships in the entire Armada - sank at the mouth of Clew Bay. These were two of twenty-six Armada ships wrecked along the Irish coast. The *Gran Grin*, carrying 329 men and 28 guns, drifted onto the rocks at Clare Island. According to English accounts, the captain and about one hundred crew made their way to safety on the island, but were killed on the orders of one of the O'Malley chieftains. The remainder of the crew were said to have drowned.

This story depends solely on one written account. Yet other versions permeated history, including one which suggested that the Spanish were anchored offshore at Clare Island for six days before the ship was wrecked by a massive storm. Another suggests that the men were taken as prisoners on the island, that dozens were killed trying to escape and the remainder handed over to the notorious Richard Bingham. Yet another story led to the belief that the *Gran Grin* was actually wrecked near the Corraun peninsula, on the north side of the bay, but was mistaken for the 26-gun *San Nicolas Prodaneli*, and that the ship's treasures were picked clean by the O'Malley and Bourke clansmen. Whatever the ensuing circumstances, it is agreed by historians that both ships sank in Clew Bay. Oddly enough, there is no mention of Granuaile or her response to any of these events.

The *Fancy*, a Man O' War vessel originally belonging to Charles II of the 1694 Spanish expedition from Corunna, but usurped by Henry Everly (Long Ben) and used for piracy, is recorded arriving at Inishlyre in June 1696 with 20 pirates on board. It is not certain what happened to the ship but it is thought to have been abandoned or wrecked.

In 1835, the 91-ton schooner *Uxbridge*, en route for Inishlyre harbour, ran ashore on the island of Inishgort at the back of the lighthouse. According to the *Evening Freeman* on Saturday 2nd.March 1835, 'the weather was so thick that the light could not be seen at the time. Immediately on the circumstance being made known, the boats belonging to the Chance and Hawk, Revenue Cruisers and the Coast

Guard boat at Inishlyre proceeded to her assistance, when the former boat with much difficulty, reached the vessel, and succeeded in rescuing the whole of her crew from a watery grave. The vessel was from Glasgow, bound for Westport and laden with coals and metal ware, and neither vessel or cargo was insured'.

In 1860, the *Leguan*, a Glasgow based 349-ton vessel was en route from Grenada to Greenock with a cargo of rum, sugar and molasses. She was caught in a gale and drifted into Clew bay. She was at risk of going ashore at Lecanvey, near Westport, so the master, William Buchanan, had the masts cut. Three pilot boats went out to the stricken vessel despite the bad weather. The men boarded the vessel but their three boats sank. The Master of *Leguan* was unable to get ashore until 6 a.m. the following day. While he was ashore trying to get an anchor and a steam tug, a fire broke out on his vessel. The fire spread rapidly so the crew, fearing there was powder on board, left the vessel. She became a total loss. An inquiry ordered at Westport found Master Buchanan at fault for anchoring when he could have gone to Inishgort. He was also blamed for going ashore when the officer left onboard was not capable of holding the vessel. The cause of the fire was not discovered. The crew of the three pilot boats were rewarded with £5 by the Merchant Mariner Fund.

In 1886, the *Spirit*, a 26-ton cutter owned by Patrick Hopkins, sank off Carrowmore Point on Clare Island. The newly built ship had been loaded with herrings, which she was not built to carry. The load subsequently broke the ship's back.

In June 1894, a vessel carrying about one hundred Achill Island 'tatie hokers' – migrant harvesters bound for Scotland – overturned when the young passengers rushed to the side to see the Glascow-bound steamer SS Elm near Westport Quay. Unable to lower the mainsail in time, the boat foundered and thirty-two people drowned.

In 1899, the 52-year old, 44-ton wooden sloop *Flora* of Westport was at anchor at Inishlyre with two crew aboard when she was hit by the schooner *Kate* of Westport in a WSW force 9 wind and she became a total loss.

In 1904, the *Pearl*, a 36-ton wooden smack, caught fire and burned in Inishlyre harbour.

The Wrecks of Clew Bay

In 1928, the 200-ton ketch Charles Stewart Parnell, which serviced the lighthouses with coal and other supplies, caught fire and sank near Inishlyre island. It now lies in twelve metres of water between Islandmore and the channel between Inishgort and Collan Beg islands. Local legend has it that there is an enormous lobster living in the ship's boiler and has been trapped in there for over thirty years, as it is too big to escape.

The Clare Island to Westport ferry Rossend was washed ashore during a storm in 1993. The bow now lies on the northern side of the island.

There are many other wrecks in the Clew Bay area, which despite the protection offered by the massive Clare Island at the head of the bay, is often at the mercy of brutal storms sweeping across the North Atlantic. This, together with the numerous shingle bars, submerged rocks and drowned drumlins around the inner bay, makes navigation around this area fraught with danger.

The Magic of Brackloon Wood

Brackloon Wood is an ancient and little-known place, not far from the remarkable Boheh Stone (where a 5,800-year old tablet was discovered in 2016). The 173-acre forest lies undisturbed and still in low hills on the eastern side of Croagh Patrick, its 200-year old Atlantic oak trees fringed with lichen and ferns. Yet these are just indicators of a much deeper past, when the entire area was covered with oak forest. This occurred after the glaciers started to recede from Ireland over 12,000 years ago, so that when the first humans arrived around three thousand years later, they found trees covering the lower lands around the more exposed mountainsides.

There are local stories of a Celtic past, of caves and monuments hidden in these woods. There are moss and bramble-covered standing stones found here. There is also a prominent ringfort and even a stone circle.

Other evidence of early human settlements is found here – several *fulacta fiadh* – a type of cooking pit constructed during the mid to late Bronze Age. These were usually constructed near streams or rivers, which provided the water to fill a stone or timber trough. Stones were heated on a nearby fire, and were then used to boil the water in the trough. Ringforts were built in Ireland during the early Christian period after 300 a.d. and were predominantly used for human habitation for hundreds of years. Earthen ringforts are called 'raths', while stone ones are referred to as 'cashels'. These had as many as three concentric lines of 'defense' in the form of walls. The ringforts were used by humans and also as a shelter for animals. The 'door' to the fort was often built on the eastern side, away from the prevailing westerly winds. The ringfort in Brackloon Wood is a Cashel, some 25 metres wide, located in the centre of the forest.

The 19th century author Thackeray called Brackloon "noble woods". At that time, they were a part of Westport House Estate, owned by the Marquis of Sligo. Patrick's Causeway or 'Tóchar Phádraig', passes close to the woods. This route predates Saint Patrick by many hundreds of years. It was believed to be a significant road capable of carrying wheeled traffic from Rathcroghan (Cruachan) in County Roscommon – home of the High Kings of Connaught and the legendary Queen Maeve – to Cruachan Aigli (now Croagh Patrick).

Evidence of extensive prehistoric settlements in this area is already indicated by the presence of cairns on the shoulders of Croagh Patrick. These large burial mounds of earth or stone are thought by Archaeologist Leo Morahan to have their origin in the late Neolithic or early Bronze Age.

Brackloon has undergone many changes in the years since it was pristine forest. Significant clearance of woodlands took place in the 16th and 17th centuries, after the invention of the blast furnace. Colonel John Browne, who had acquired huge swathes of land in Ireland, built what is now referred to as Westport House and established an ironworks at the nearby village of Knappagh in 1687. At its peak, 150 men were employed in the making of cannonballs, iron and metal tools to British garrisons in Galway and the island of Inishbofin. The ironworks was fueled by charcoal produced from local timber. Much of the deforestation of Ireland occurred during the industrial age, when the country's English overlords used the country as a source for timber and charcoal. This exploitation of woodland occurred over centuries, and later fast-growing conifers were introduced. These 'intruders' to the primeval forest were culled by the Forest Service in the late 1990s, as the State sought to restore it to its deciduous origins by planting oaks, birches, willows and ash trees.

The Southern Wilderness

As a pilgrim approaches the shoulder of Croagh Patrick on a clear day, waves of mountain ranges stretch towards the southern horizon.

There is only one village of any size in the thirty spectacular kilometres between the Reek and Leenane, the gateway to Connemara. This is Drummin (*An Dromainn*, meaning "The Ridge"). It was also on this plain between Croagh Patrick and the next mountain ranges of Partry and Sheeffry that a young nun, Sister Irene Gibson, lived in a forest home as a hermit for several years up to 2003, in an unsuccessful attempt to set up a hermitage near the village.

It is said that after Saint Patrick fasted on the Reek for forty days, he threw a silver bell down the south side of the mountain knocking the she-demon Corra from the sky into a lake, sited at the base of the mountain and known locally as Lough na Corra.

Looking southwest from the Reek, the first mountain range that comes into view is that of the Sheeffry Hills (*Cnoic Shíofra*, meaning "Hills of the Wraith"). This desolate and remote ridge affords spectacular views of both the Reek and the magnificent ranges to the south and west, including the Mweelrea group, the Maumturks, Ben Gorm, Devilsmother, and the Twelve Bens of Connemara. The highest peak, Barrclashcame, is eight metres higher than the summit of the Reek.

Looking southwest from the top of the Reek, one can see the deep gorge that forms the break between Connaught Province's highest mountain, Mweelrea (813 metres), and the Sheeffry Hills. This is the valley of Doolough (*Dubh Lough* – The Black Lake). This beautiful valley was once the scene of tragedy during the great famine, when starving residents were forced to walk for many miles in winter conditions to request certification as paupers from the authorities who were dining in Delphi Lodge, at the southern end of the lake. The commonly accepted story is that they were refused audience and instructed to return the following morning. After a brutally cold night, the residents acquired their certifications, then set off towards the town of Louisburgh, some twelve miles distant. Several were too weak to continue and fell by the side of the road, where their bodies were later collected. Today, the monument in Doolough valley has an inscription from Mahatma Gandhi: "How can men feel themselves honoured by the humiliation of their fellow beings?"

Beyond Doolough is Ireland's only fjord – Killary Harbour. On a fine day, the Killary is visible from the Reek, as are the beautiful Twelve Bens and the tooth-like mountains of Maumturk.

There are no direct roads from the Reek to the mountains of Mayo and Connemara. By car, it is necessary to either go via Westport or Louisburgh. The *Western Way* hiking trail does cross the valley, however, and intrepid walkers can follow this path without fear of motorized traffic.

The area south of Croagh Patrick seems placid today, but as evidenced by tales from Patrick's Causeway, which joins the main pilgrimage trail up the mountain from the southern side, this region has many stories of great hardship and persecution from not so long ago.

The Drowned Drumlins

Clew Bay extends eastwards from Clare Island towards the towns of Newport and Westport. The eastern end of the bay is divided into Westport Bay to the south, and Newport Bay to the north.

As outlined in this book, there are well over one hundred named 'islands' in Clew Bay. These are usually referred to as 'drowned' drumlins, even though their tops are still visible at high water mark. However, there are also a significant amount of truly 'drowned' drumlins beneath the waters of this spectacular bay.

The name drumlin is derived from the Irish word, droiroimnín (littlest ridge). Drumlins are typically aligned parallel to one another. A drumlin may be defined as *"An elongated hill, streamlined in the direction of ice flow and composed largely of glacial deposits"*. Basically, the glacier pushes up and over debris that the ice is moving forward. Many of the Clew Bay drumlins are steepest on the upstream (west or northwestern side) and trail off toward the east or southeast. The drumlins of Clew Bay were inundated by the waters of the Atlantic Ocean after the glacial ice melted.

The drumlins of Clew Bay are also referred to as a 'swarm', as there are many in a small area. This is also known as a 'basket of eggs' topography. The drumlins of this bay are composed of boulder clay. Some of the westward facing boulder cliffs of the islands are close to one hundred feet high.

The area around Moynish More has only four other named islands but many hidden drowned drumlins that lie in between 5-10 metres of water (partial representation derived from the InfoMar undersea surveys of 2002-2003).

The Drowned Drumlins

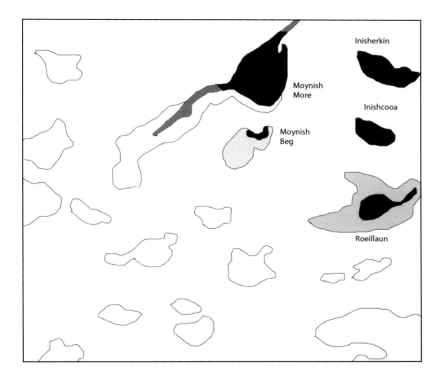

- ■ Visible at High Water Mark
- ▨ Shingle Bar
- ▢ Less than 5 metres of water
- ▢ Less than 10 metres of water

Birds Found on Clew Bay Islands

The following are some examples of birds that may be seen on or around the Clew Bay islands:

Barnacle Goose	Herring Gull	Dunlin
Bar-tailed Godwit	Common Tern	Great Northern Diver
Widgeon	Cormorant	Greenshank
Brent Goose	Curlew	Grey Heron

34

Birds sighted on the Islands*

Arctic Skua
Barnacle Goose
Bar-tailed Godwit
Black Duck
Black-backed gull
Common Tern
Cormorant
Dunlin
Fulmar
Glaucous Gull
Glossy Ibis
Golden Plover
Great Northern Diver
Great Skua
Greenshank
Herring Gull
Iceland Gull
Little Gull
Manx Shearwater
Osprey
Oyster Catcher
Puffin
Redshank
Sandwich Tern
Spoonbill
Whooper Swan
Widgeon

source – http://www.irishbirding.com

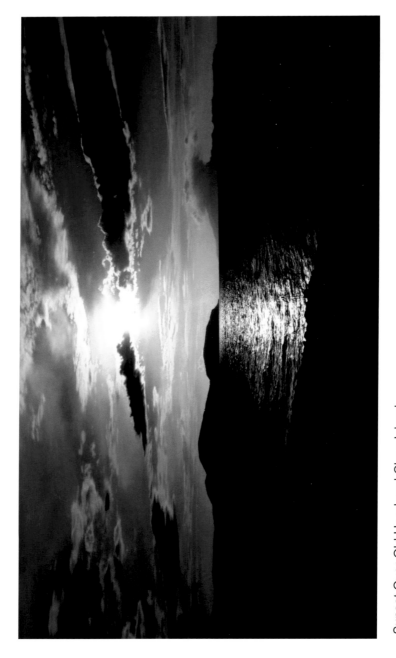

Sunset Over Old Head and Clare Island

Winter dawn around Croagh Patrick from Lecanvey Pier

View from Knockmore on Clare Island with Inishturk in the distance

Westport Bay from the main road near Belclare

The Reek as seen from the summit of Barrclashcame in the Sheeffry Hills

Croagh Patrick and the Islands of Clew Bay

Tóchar Phádraig near Aughagower, with Croagh Patrick in the background

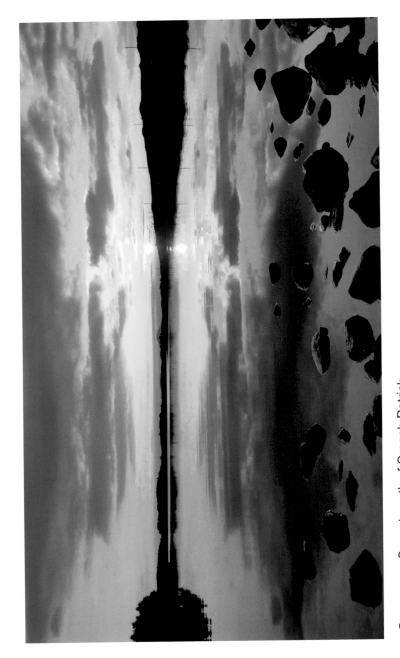

Connemara Sunset south of Croagh Patrick

Croagh Patrick and the Islands of Clew Bay

Rockfleet (Also known as Carrickhowley) – last home of Granuaile

Croagh Patrick from the island of Collan More

Croagh Patrick and the Islands of Clew Bay

On the edge of Brackloon Wood

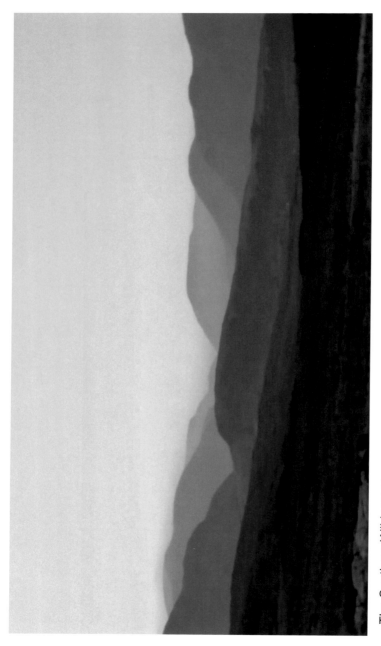

The Southern Wilderness

The Reek in Winter

Illanoona Island, looking towards Moynish More

Annagh Island from east Croagh Patrick

Illanroe Island near Westport on a foggy morning

Croagh Patrick and the Islands of Clew Bay

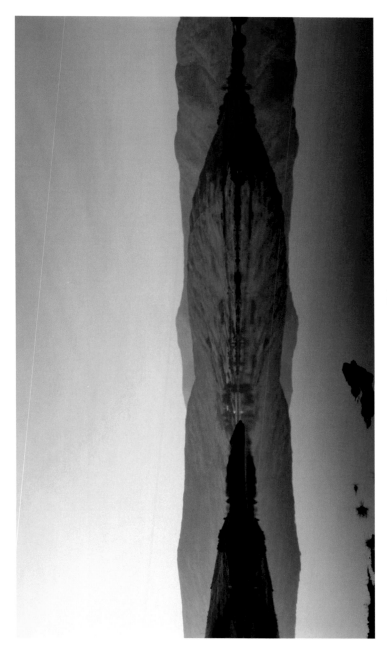

Killary Harbour is situated on the edge of the Southern Wilderness

Croagh Patrick from Old Head Beach

Inishlyre Harbour – deep enough to be used by larger ships

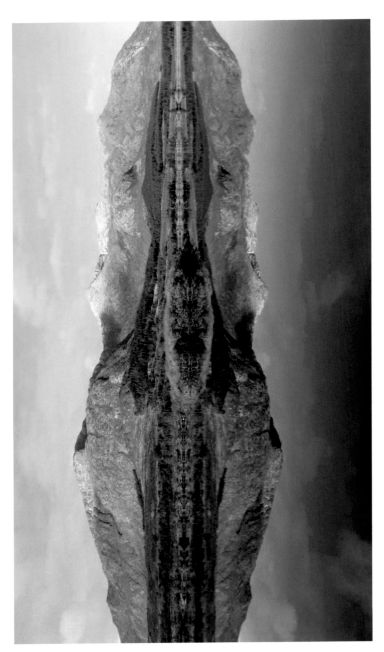

The Twelve Bens are visible from the Reek on a clear day

Clew Bay and its Surroundings

Clew Bay is located on the west coast of Ireland, approximately 250 kilometres from Dublin and 80 kilometres northwest of Galway.

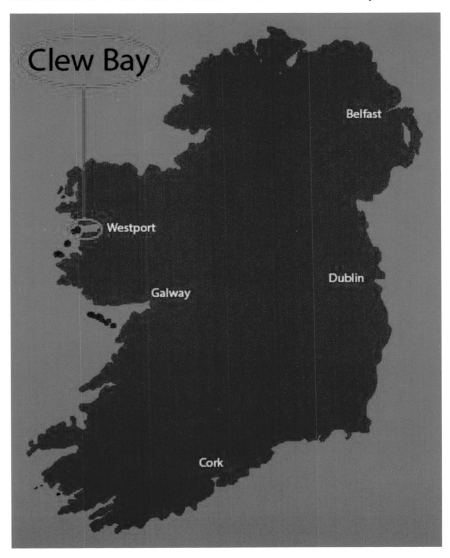

Clew Bay extends west from the mainland towns of Newport and Westport to Clare Island. The islands of Inishturk, Inishbofin, Inishshark, Cahir and Achillbeg, shown in the map below, are not part of Clew Bay, but are described in this book (see the section entitled "Clare Island and the Outlying Islands").

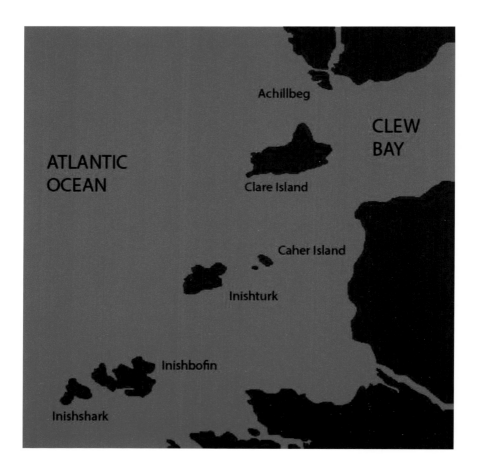

Clew Bay Overview

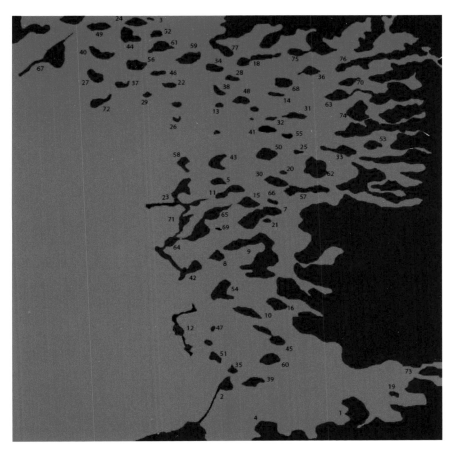

Islands two acres and over in size. See next pages for key to names.

Not shown - Illanoona

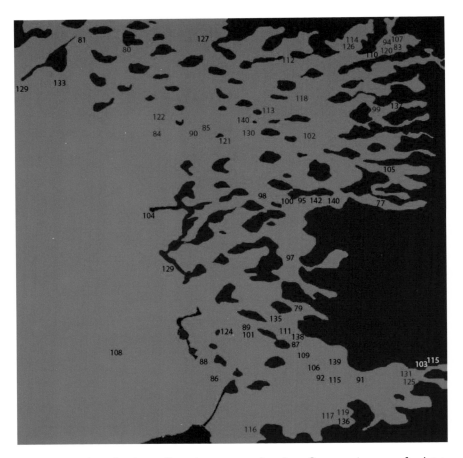

Islands and rocks less than two acres in size. See next pages for key to names.

Not shown – Smaller Islands and Rocks of Clare Island (Calliaghcrom Rock, Kinadevdilla, Mweelaun)

Clew Bay Overview

Westport Bay as seen from Croagh Patrick

Some of the distinctive drumlin islands in Newport Bay

The Larger Islands

1. Annagh (East, Middle & West)
2. Bartraw
3. Beetle Island North
4. Cahernaran
5. Calf Island
6. Clare Island
7. Clynish
8. Collan Beg
9. Collan More
10. Crovinish
11. Derrinish
12. Dorinish (More and Beg)
13. Freaghillan West
14. Freaghillanluggagh
15. Freaghillan
16. Illanataggart
17. Illanoona
18. Illannambraher (East & West)
19. Illanroe
20. Illannaconney
21. Illaunnamona
22. Inishacrick
23. Inishbee
24. Inishbobunnan
25. Inishbollog
26. Inishcannon
27. Inishcooa
28. Inishcoragh
29. Inishcorky
30. Inishcottle
31. Inishcuill
32. Inishcuill West
33. Inishdaff
34. Inishdasky
35. Inishdaugh
36. Inishdaweel
37. Inishdeash More
38. Inishdoonver
39. Inisheeny
40. Inisherkin

41. Inishfesh
42. Inishgort
43. Inishgowla (near Inishoo)
44. Inishgowla (near Inishbobunnan)
45. Inishgowla South
46. Inishilra
47. Inishimmel
48. Inishkee
49. Inishkeel
50. Inishlaughil
51. Inishleague
52. Inishlim
53. Inishloy
54. Inishlyre
55. Inishmolt
56. Inishnacross
57. Inishnakillew
58. Inishoo
59. Inishquirk
60. Inishraher
61. Inishtubbrid
62. Inishturk Beg
63. Inishturlin
64. Island More
65. Knockycahillaun
66. Moneybeg
67. Moynish More
68. Muckinish
69. Quinsheen
70. Rabbit Island (Newport)
71. Rabbit Island (Island More)
72. Roeillaun
73. Roman Island
74. Rosbarnagh
75. Roslynagh
76. Rosmore
77. Rosturk

The Smaller Islands and Rocks

78. Atticlea (located in a channel east of Inishnakillew)
79. Beetle Island (located east of Illanataggart)
80. Beetle Island South (located SW of Inishgowla)
81. Black Rock (located northeast of Moynish More)
82. Calliaghcrom Rock (located just north of Clare Island)
83. Camel Island (located ESE of Forillan, near Illanavrick)
84. Carrickachaash (two locations south of Inishcorky)
85. Carrickachorra (located northwest of Illanmaw)
86. Carrickatraha (located just west of Bartraw)
87. Carrickawart Island (located east of Inishgowla South)
88. Carricklahan (rocks located just south of Dorinish Beg)
89. Carricknaguroge (located west of Inishgowla South)
90. Carricklahan (rocks located south of Inishcannon)
91. Carricknacaly (located south of Pigeon Point)
92. Carricknamore (located south east of Corillan)
93. Carrickwee (located east of Inishlaghan)
94. Carrigeenaskibbole (located east of Burrishoole Channel)
95. Carrigeenglass (south of Inishnakillew)
96. Carrigeenglass North (located just south of Inishnakillew)
97. Carrigeenglass South (strip of rocks located east of Collan More)
98. Carrigeennafrankagh (located northeast of Freaghillan)
99. Carrigeennaronty (located east of Rosbarnagh Island)
100. Carrigeenrevagh (near Trawbaun, west of Carrigeenglass North)
101. Carricknaguroge (located west of Inishgowla South)
102. Carrickwee (located east of Inishlaghan)
103. Cleavlagh Strand (north of Westport Channel)
104. Cloghcormick (located west of Inishbee)
105. Corragaun (located on an inlet east of Inishturk Beg)
106. Corillan ("The Scotsman's Bonnet" near Inishraher)
107. Corragaunnagalliaghdoo (east of Burrishoole Channel)
108. Creggandillisk (located west of Bartraw)
109. Finnaun Island (located northeast of Inishraher)
110. Forillan (one located east of Burrishoole Channel)
111. Forillan (one located east of Inishgowla South)
112. Forillanabraher (located east of Illannambraher East))
113. Freaghillan East (located between Inishcuill West and Inishkee)

114. Gobfadda (located on Luggatallan Strand, north of Kid Island East)
115. Green Islands (located on Cleavlagh Strand)
116. Illannaglaur (located south of Cahernaran Island)
117. Illanakishta (located west of Roeillan, near Annagh Island)
118. Illanascraw (located east of Freaghillanluggagh)
119. Illanatee (located just east of Annagh Island)
120. Illanavrick (located east of Burrishoole Channel)
121. Illanmaw (located north of Inishoo in Newport Bay)
122. Inishdeashbeg (located southwest of Inishilra)
123. Inisheanmore Rock (located south of Inishcannon)
124. Inishlaghan (north of Inishimmel and east of Dorinish More)
125. Inishmweela (located near Roman Island)
126. Kid Island East (located south of Gobfadda)
127. Kid Island West (located northeast of Inishquirk)
128. Kinadevdilla (located at the southwestern end of Clare Island)
129. Malmore (located south of Moynish More)
130. Mauherillan (located southwest of Inishfesh)
131. Monkelly's Rocks (north of the entrance to Westport Harbour)
132. Moynish (on a bar between Inishgort and Island More)
133. Moynish Beg (located just south of Moynish More)
134. Mweelaun (located south of Clare Island and west of Roonagh)
135. Rocky Island (located south of Illanataggart)
136. Roeillan (located just south of Annagh Island)
137. Sixpenny Island (located in the Teevmore Channel)
138. Sloe Island (located east of Inishgowla South)
139. Stony Island (located east of Finnaun Island, in Westport Bay)
140. Taash Island (located west of Inishcuill West)
141. Toby's Rock (near Trawbaun, off Inishnakillew)
142. Trawbaun (shallow water around Inishnakillew)

*As noted in this book, there are several small unnamed islands and rocks in the Clew Bay area. This list represents those identified for ordnance survey purposes.

Islands of Clew Bay by Section

Inner Clew Bay can be more or less divided into four sections, consisting of those islands in the northwest, the inner islands of Newport Bay, Westport Bay, and the 'middle' islands that border these two bays.

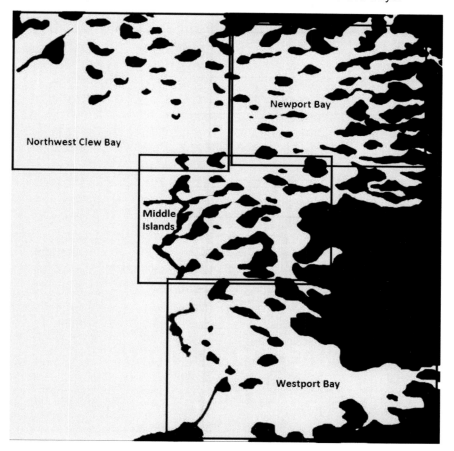

Not shown – Clare Island and outlying large islands beyond Clew Bay are described in the last section of this book.

Islands of Clew Bay by Section (continued)

The Middle Islands	Inner Newport Bay	Northwest Clew Bay	Westport Bay
Calf Island	Freaghillan	Beetle North	Annagh
Clynish	Iuggagh	Freaghillan West	Bartraw
Collan Beg	Illannambraher	Illanoona	Cahernaran
Collan More	Inishbollog	Inishacrick	Crovinish
Derrinish	Inishcoragh	Inishbobunnan	Dorinish
Freaghillan	Inishcuill	Inishcannon	Illanataggart
Illannaconney	Inishcuill West	Inishcooa	Illanroe
Illaunnamona	Inishdaff	Inishcorky	Inishdaugh
Inishbee	Inishdaweel	Inishdasky	Inisheeny
Inishcottle	Inishfesh	Inishdeash More	Inishgowla South
Inishgort	Inishkee	Inishdoonver	Inishimmel
Inishnakillew	Inishlaughil	Inisherkin	Inishleague
Inishturk Beg	Inishloy	Inishgowla	Inishlyre
Island More	Inishmolt	Inishgowla	Inishraher
Knockycahillaun	Inishturlin	Inishilra	Roman
Moneybeg	Muckinish	Inishkeel	
Quinsheen	Rabbit Island	Inishlim	
Rabbit (Island More)	Rosbarnagh	Inishnacross	
	Roslynagh	Inishoo	
	Rosmore	Inishquirk	
	Rosturk	Inishtubbrid	
		Moynish More	
		Roeillaun	

The Middle Islands

The Middle Islands at the heart of Clew Bay are dominated by Collan More, Clynish and the enormous shingle bars around Island More and its neighbours.

- Calf Island
- Clynish
- Collan Beg
- Collan More
- Derrinish
- Freaghillan
- Illannaconney
- Illaunnamona
- Inishbee
- Inishcottle
- Inishgort
- Inishnakillew
- Inishturk Beg
- Island More
- Knockycahillaun
- Moneybeg
- Quinsheen
- Rabbit (off Island More)

NOTE - The 'middle' islands of Clew Bay are best seen by taking side roads off the N59 (starting with the signpost for Saint Brendan's Sports Club/Seapoint House about 7 kilometres south of Newport, towards Westport) and ending with the signpost for Roscahill Pier, about 5 kilometres north of Westport.

The Middle Islands

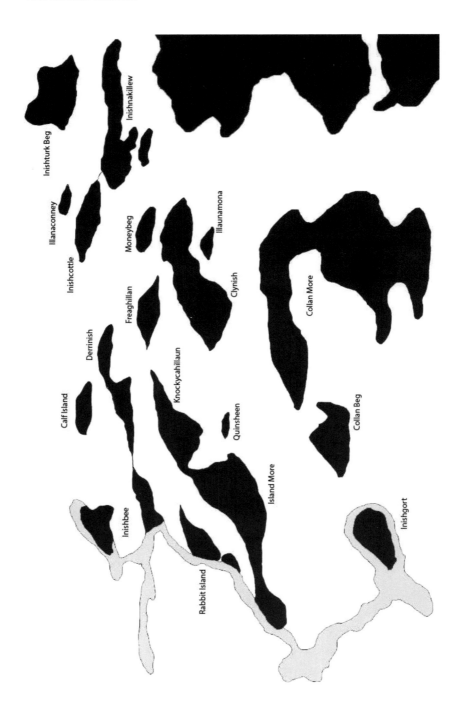

Calf Island

Latitude: 53°51'10"N
Longitude: 9°39'14"W

Normal Grid Ref = L 911 905
10-digit Grid Ref = L 91140 90542

8 acres (58th Largest Island in Clew Bay)
Highest Point: 23 metres/76 feet (50th Highest)

Calf Island (Oileán na Gamhna) is an uninhabited island situated south of Inishgowla and east of Inishbee. It is visible from the mainland at the western point Inishnakillew, looking west northwest (to the right of the larger island of Derrinish).

Calf Island was once leased from the Marquis of Sligo by the Reverent Giles Eyre. This man had a 'glebe' (a piece of land serving as part of a clergyman's benefice and providing income) of six acres on the island, but no house. It is now used for sheep grazing. The tidal flow is particularly strong on the north side of the island, as it narrows between the island and Inishgowla.

Clynish

Latitude: 53°50'35"N
Longitude: 9°38'9"W

Normal Grid Ref = L 921 894
10-digit Grid Ref = L 92188 89446

80 acres (3rd Largest Island in Clew Bay)
Highest Point: 138 feet/42 metres (8th Highest)

Clynish (Claidhnis – Island of the Ditch) is a large private island situated north of its even larger neighbour Collan More and south of Freaghillan.

It can be seen from the mainland at Roscahill, about nine kilometres from Westport (turn left off the N59 after about five kilometres).

Clynish is one of a few islands in Clew Bay currently inhabited. In 1841 there were 87 people living on Clynish – a total of 16 families. In 1911, twenty-three people lived in three dwellings. By 2006, there were just five inhabitants. The island is only accessible by boat. In 2003, the National Development Plan (NDP) and Mayo County Council agreed to build a three-hundred-thousand-euro pier on Clynish, which allows a motor boat to land even during the Clew Bay winter weather.

Collan Beg

Latitude: 53°49'58"N
Longitude: 9°39'18"W

Normal Grid Ref = L 910 883
10-digit Grid Ref = L 91065 88305

16 acres (42nd Largest Island in Clew Bay)
Highest Point: 83 feet/25 metres (45th Highest)

Collan Beg (Collainn Bheag – Small Heather Island) is an uninhabited island (although it has a private cabin on the east beach) situated southwest of Collan More and northeast of Inishgort.

Although Collan Beg was not listed as being inhabited in 1841, in 1861 a family of nine lived there, and the census of 1911 shows that a John Malley lived there in a thatched two room cottage with his wife Mary and 75-year old mother Anne. The island is now the abode of livestock.

Collan More

Latitude: 53°49'57"N
Longitude: 9°38'23"W

Normal Grid Ref = L 924 880
10-digit Grid Ref = L 92459 88098

199 acres (2nd Largest Island in Clew Bay)
Highest Point: 174 feet/53 metres (2nd Highest)

Collan More (Collainn Mhór – formerly Cuileann or Big Holly Island) is a large inhabited island situated just northwest of Rosmoney Pier. It can also be seen from the mainland at Roscahill, about nine kilometres from Westport (left off the N59 after about five kilometres and about three kilometres west).

Collan More was inhabited by 213 people in 1841. In 1911, it included Collanmore National School and nine private dwellings occupied by forty people. By 2006, there were just eighteen inhabitants and the school had closed (although it has been recently renovated, but not used as a school). Today, the island is the home of a sailing school that can accommodate more than fifty people.

Derrinish

Latitude: 53°50'59"N
Longitude: 9°39'4"W

Normal Grid Ref = L 913 902
10-digit Grid Ref = L 91353 90210

29 acres (21st Largest Island in Clew Bay)
Highest Point: 72 feet/22 metres (55th Highest)

Derrinish (Dairinis – formerly Doire Inis or Oakwood Island) is an uninhabited island situated northeast of Island More and west of

Inishcottle. In 1841, there were forty inhabitants on the island, a number which dropped to seven members of the Thomas Gaven family living in a two-room thatched cottage in 1911. By 2006, there was just one inhabitant on the island.

Derrinish can be clearly viewed from the western tip of Inishcottle (reachable from Inishnakillew by a causeway). The island is connected to Inishbee by a shingle bar.

Freaghillan

Latitude: 53°50'49"N
Longitude: 9°38'27"W

Normal Grid Ref = L 920 898
10-digit Grid Ref = L 92017 89879

19 acres (39th Largest Island in Clew Bay)
Highest Point: 87 feet/26 metres (42nd)

Freaghillan (Fhraochoileáin or Heather Island) is an uninhabited island situated just north of Clynish and east of Knockycahillaun Island. The only record of people having lived on Freaghillan was in 1861, when a family of eight people lived in one house. It has been uninhabited ever since.

Illannaconney

Latitude: 53°51'19"N
Longitude: 9°37'30"W

Normal Grid Ref = L 930 907
10-digit Grid Ref = L 93055 90768

4 acres (68th Largest Island in Clew Bay)
Highest Point: 46 feet/14 metres (67th)

Illannaconney (Oileán an Chonnaidh – apparently Firewood Island, despite its similarity to the Irish translation of Rabbit) is an uninhabited island situated between Inishlaughil and Inishcottle Island, and is nearby to Inishturk Beg. Illannaconney is best viewed from Inishcottle, which is accessible by road. Census records from the 1800's indicate that even before the famine years, Illannaconney was not inhabited.

Illaunnamona

Latitude: 53°50'32"N
Longitude: 9°37'56"W

Normal Grid Ref = L 924 893
10-digit Grid Ref = L 92481 89383

4 acres (69th Largest Island in Clew Bay)
Highest Point: 36 feet/11 metres (67th)

Illaunnamona (Island of the Bog) is a small, uninhabited island situated beside Clynish and north of Collan More. There are no records of Illaunnamona ever being inhabited.

Inishbee

Latitude: 53°50'58"N
Longitude: 9°40'2"W

Normal Grid Ref = L 901 903
10-digit Grid Ref = L 90113 90346

51 acres (11th Largest Island in Clew Bay)
Highest Point: 102 feet/29 metres (24th)

Inishbee (Inis Buidhe – Yellow Island) is situated just north of Island More and south of Inishoo. It is sometimes considered a double island along with Derrinish, and at low tide is connected to its southern neighbours.

Although it is uninhabited now, in 1911 there were ten people in two families living on the island of Inishbee. Prior to the famine, Inishbee was the property of Sir Samuel O'Malley, who owned several islands in the baronies of Burrishoole and Murrisk. By all accounts, O'Malley was in serious financial difficulties after the famine and sold these properties – as well as Clare Island - to the Irish Life Assurance Society.

Inishcottle

Latitude: 53°51'10"N
Longitude: 9°37'43"W

Normal Grid Ref = L 928 905
10-digit Grid Ref = L 92834 90508

23 acres (33rd Largest island in Clew Bay)
Highest Point: 90 feet/27 metres (39th)

Inishcottle Island (Inis Coitil – Cottle's Island) is an inhabited island located northwest of Inishnakillew. It is connected to this island by a causeway. In 1911, there were five two room houses on the island, occupied by forty-four members of the Quinn and O'Malley families, nineteen of whom were aged less than ten.

Inishgort

Latitude: 53°49'43"N
Longitude: 9°39'58"W

Normal Grid Ref = L 904 879
10-digit Grid Ref = L 90413 87993

21 acres (34th largest island in Clew Bay)
Highest Point: 105 feet/32 metres (20th)

Inishgort Island (Inis Goirt – Field Island) is an inhabited island located close to the mouth of Westport Bay. It boasts the only working lighthouse in the bay and is currently inhabited by one individual who resides in a cottage on the east side of the island, with a pier facing Collan Beg. That inhabitant is the former postmaster for Clew Bay bringing mail from the mainland to the inhabited islands. In 1911, there were three inhabited houses on the island, but unusually, these were inhabited by only seven adults aged between twenty-seven and seventy-eight. At low tide, access is possible via a shingle bar from nearby Island More.

Inishnakillew

Latitude: 53° 50' 52" N
Longitude: 9° 36' 57" W

Normal Grid Ref = L 936 902
10-digit Grid Ref = L 93652 90219

58 acres (8th largest island in Clew Bay)
Highest Point: 96 feet/29 metres (33rd)

Inishnakillew Island (Inis na Coilleadh) is an inhabited island located in Newport Bay. It is connected to the mainland by a causeway. In 1911, the island had seven houses occupied by thirty-four people. Five of these houses belonged to the Quinn family, including one house with seven teenage boys and girls, and another with three generations living together.

Inishturk Beg

Latitude: 53°51'25"N
Longitude: 9°36'38"W

Normal Grid Ref = L 940 909
10-digit Grid Ref = L 94035 90909

59 acres (7th largest island in Clew Bay)
Highest Point: 173 feet/53 metres (3rd)

Inishturk Beg Island (Inis Torc Beg – Small Island of the Boar) is an inhabited island situated in Newport Bay.

In 1911, Mary Berry lived in a two room house on the southeast side of Inishturk Beg with her three children. In later years, the island was purchased by Nadim Sadek, a millionaire who spent an estimated ten million dollars to develop it as a high end private retreat. Today, there are five houses on the island. Mary Berry's original cottage on the island is now a spacious two-storey structure with three bedrooms and three reception rooms, overlooking the original pier.

Island More

Latitude: 53°50'23"N
Longitude: 9°39'51"W

Normal Grid Ref = L 905 890
10-digit Grid Ref = L 90528 89022

77 acres (4th largest island in Clew Bay)
Highest Point: 72 feet/22 metres (56th)

Island More (an tOileán Mór) is an uninhabited island situated near the mouth of Westport Bay. This is the largest of a number of connected islands, including (at low tide) Inish Gort to the west, Knockycahillaun and Freaghillan to the northeast, and the inhabited island of Clynish to the east. Rabbit Island to the northwest is also joined to Derrinish and Inishbee, and there is a connecting spit to Quinsheen Island also. Rabbit Island has had cattle living on it in recent years. There are still six houses on the island, situated in a sheltered gap between Island More and Knockycahillaun. There is a laneway though the gap. In 1911, there were four houses on Island More. Each of these houses had two rooms. At the time there were twenty-seven inhabitants.

Knockycahillaun

Latitude: 53°50'73"N
Longitude: 9°39'21"W

Normal Grid Ref = L 909 895
10-digit Grid Ref = L 90988 89581

34 acres (14th largest island in Clew Bay)
Highest Point: 119 feet/36 metres (14th)

Knockycahillaun Island (Cnoc Uí Chathaláin) is an uninhabited island situated in Newport Bay. It is really an extension of Island More. In 1911, there were four inhabited houses on the island with sixteen occupants from the Kelly, Gill and Moore families. Mary Moore, age 71, lived alone, while Joseph Kelly (age 68) and his wife Ellen (62), shared their house with sister-in-law Mary Gill (74).

Moneybeg

Latitude: 53°50'51"N
Longitude: 9°37'48"W

Normal Grid Ref = L 927 899
10-digit Grid Ref = L 92736 89918

9 acres (57th largest island in Clew Bay)
Highest Point: 56 feet (65th)

Moneybeg Island (An Muine Beag) is a small, uninhabited island situated west of Inishnakillew and north of Clynish, on the edge of Newport Bay.

Quinsheen

Latitude: 53°50'25"N
Longitude: 9°39'15"W

Normal Grid Ref = L 901 886
10-digit Grid Ref = L 90107 88666

2 acres (81st largest island in Clew Bay)
Highest Point: 30 feet/9 metres (74th)

Quinsheen Island (Cuinsín – Little Snub Nose) is a small, uninhabited island located just east of Island More. There is a pontoon on the spit that joins with Island More.

Rabbit (Island More)

Latitude: 53°50'29"N
Longitude: 9°40'8"W

Normal Grid Ref = L 900 893
10-digit Grid Ref = L 90095 89360

20 acres (28th largest island in Clew Bay)
Highest Point: 72 feet/22 metres (57th)

Rabbit Island (Oileán na gCoinín) is an uninhabited island situated just west of Island More and south of Inishbee. It is connected to both these neighbours by shingle bars.

Inner Newport Bay

Inner Newport Bay includes all of the islands east of the Rosturk peninsula and north of Inish Turk Beg.

Although not part of Clew Bay, Furnace Lough, which flows into the Burrishoole Channel, north of Rosmore in Newport Bay, boasts three islands – Inishower, Illanroe and Saints Island.

- Freaghillanluggagh
- Illannambraher
- Inishbollog
- Inishcoragh
- Inishcuill
- Inishcuill West
- Inishdaff
- Inishdaweel
- Inishfesh
- Inishkee
- Inishlaughil
- Inishloy
- Inishmolt
- Inishturlin
- Muckinish
- Rabbit (Newport Bay)
- Rosbarnagh
- Roslynagh
- Rosmore
- Rosturk

NOTE - The islands of Inner Newport Bay are best seen from side roads off the N59 (starting with the turn for Rossanrubble and Carrowbeg on the Westport Road) for the southern islands and between Newport and Rossyvera (take the turn for Carrickhowley Castle for the northern islands)

Freaghillanluggagh

Latitude: 53° 52' 35" north
Longitude: 9° 37' 39.6" west

Normal Grid Ref = L 928 931
10-digit Grid Ref = L 92871 93139

3 acres (72nd Largest Island in Clew Bay)
Highest Point: 65 feet/20 metres (61st)

Freaghillanluggagh (Fraochoileán Logach – Hollow of the Heather Island) is an uninhabited island in Newport Bay situated between Inishcuill and Illannambraher, close to Muckinish Island. Despite having one of the longest names, it is one of the smallest islands in the bay.

Illannambraher

Latitude: 53°53'10"N
Longitude: 9°38'1"W

Normal Grid Ref = L 921 942
10-digit Grid Ref = L 92176 94208

Illannambraher East
14 acres (47th Largest Island in Clew Bay). Highest Point: 83 feet/25 metres (46th)

Illannambraher West
11 acres (55th Largest Island in Clew Bay). Highest Point: 82 feet/25 metres (47th)

Illannambraher (Oileán na mBráthar – Island of the Brethren) is an uninhabited island situated west of Roslynagh in Newport Bay. It could be considered a group of three islands, with west and east separated by a narrow strip of land, and the tiny Forillanabraher island almost cut off on the eastern end.

To get a close view of the east island, take the N59 towards Mulranny and turn left at the sign on the main road for the refurbished Carrickhowley Castle (also called Carraigahowley or Rockfleet Castle), which is associated with the 'Pirate Queen' Grace O'Malley. Follow the road as far south as possible (it ends up on the Rossyvera peninsula). As far as records go, these islands have never been inhabited. Roslynagh offers the best view of the Forillanabraher island at the eastern tip, and Rosturk Island provides an excellent view of the Illanambraher West.

Inishbollog

Latitude: 53°51'39"N
Longitude: 9°37'6"W

Normal Grid Ref = L 934 913
10-digit Grid Ref = L 93486 91378

3 acres (73rd Largest island in Clew Bay)
Highest Point: 66 feet/20 metres (58th)

Inishbollog (Inis Bolg – Island of the Belly) is an uninhabited island situated in Newport Bay, between Inishmolt and Inishturk Beg. There are stairs from the east side to the highest point on the island.

Inishcoragh

Latitude: 53°52'51"N
Longitude: 9°38'51"W

Normal Grid Ref = L 916 936
10-digit Grid Ref = L 91616 93661

Inner Newport Bay

Normal Grid Ref = L 916 936
10-digit Grid Ref = L 91647 93646

8 acres (59th largest island in Clew Bay)
Highest Point: 79 feet/24 metres (49th)

Inishcoragh Island (Inis Córach – Pleasant Island) is an uninhabited island located in Newport Bay. It is situated due south of the Rosturk peninsula, northeast of Inishdoonver. There is a modern house on the island accessed by a path from the jetty on the northeastern side.

Inishcuill

Latitude: 53°52'14"N
Longitude: 9°37'15"W

Normal Grid Ref = L 934 924
10-digit Grid Ref = L 93456 92483

14 acres (38th largest island in Clew Bay)
Highest Point: 94 feet/28 metres (35th)

Inishcuill Island (Inish Coill – Wood Island) is an uninhabited island located in Newport Bay. It is due west of Rosbarnagh Island. In 1855, it was leased for land usage by a Michael Keane, but it does not appear to have been inhabited at any point over the past two centuries.

The island has been recognized as a resting site for harbour seals and one of several adjacent islands (Inishmolt, Inishfesh and Freaghillanluggagh) these animals are said to frequent.

Inishcuill West

Latitude: 53°52'12"N
Longitude: 9°37'50"W

Normal Grid Ref = L 927 924
10-digit Grid Ref = L 92731 92421

2 acres (80th largest island in Clew Bay)
Highest Point: TBD

Inishcuill West Island (Inis Coill Thiar – West Island of the Wood) is a small uninhabited island located in Newport Bay. It is located west of Inishcuill island and south of Freaghillanluggagh. There is no record of this island ever being inhabited. As in the case of its larger neighbour Inishcuill, it was leased for land use from landowner Judith O'Donnell by Michael Moran in the mid-19th century.

Inishdaff

Latitude: 53°51'40"N
Longitude: 9°36'2"W

Normal Grid Ref = L 948 914
10-digit Grid Ref = L 94883 91403

32 acres (16th largest island in Clew Bay)
Highest Point: 101 feet/31 metres (26th)

Inishdaff Island (Inis Damh – Ox Island), formerly Inishduff, is a relatively large uninhabited island located just offshore in Newport Bay. It is situated just west of Inishloy and the Rosbeg peninsula, and north of Inishturk Beg.

The ruins of an ancient church and graveyard are located at the eastern tip of the island, as well as evidence of some recent local burials. Trees have also been planted in this location. Several families were evicted from this island during the great famine.

In the early 19th century, Hugh O'Donnell, his wife Molly and their ten children lived on Inishdaff island. Hugh was a twelfth generation descendant of the famous Red Hugh O'Donnell (1572-1602), who had led a rebellion against the English government.

Inishdaweel

Latitude: 53°52'59"N
Longitude: 9°36'46"W

Normal Grid Ref = L 939 938
10-digit Grid Ref = L 93949 93818

15 acres (44th largest island in Clew Bay)
Highest Point: 128 feet/39 metres (10th)

Inishdaweel Island (Inis Dá Mhaol – translated by some as 'Island of the Two Bald Hills' and others as 'Island of the Two Hornless Cows') is an uninhabited island located in Newport Bay. It is a breeding ground for harbour seals and is situated due west of Rosmore Point and northeast of Muckinish Island. In the mid-19th century, it was owned by Sir Roger Palmer and leased for land by John Buchanan. There are no known records of any inhabitants on this island.

Inishfesh

Latitude: 53°52'1"N
Longitude: 9°37'56"W

Normal Grid Ref = L 926 921
10-digit Grid Ref = L 92605 92108

12 acres (52nd Largest island in Clew Bay)
Highest Point: 85 feet/26 metres

Inishfesh Island (Inis Feise – Festival Island) is an uninhabited island located in Newport Bay. It is located west of Rossanrubble Point, north of Inishlaughil. This island includes old ruins and a more recent colourful building that appears to be abandoned.

Inishkee

Latitude: 53°52'30"N
Longitude: 9°38'40"W

Normal Grid Ref = L 918 929
10-digit Grid Ref = L 91863 92987

12 acres (53rd Largest island in Clew Bay)
Highest Point: 46 feet/14 feet (68th)

Inishkee Island (Inis Caoich), is an uninhabited island located in Newport Bay, in the middle of a cluster of small islands well offshore. It may be seen from the tip of Rosturk, looking directly south beyond the nearby Inishcoragh, to the left of Inishdoonver. There are no records of this island ever being inhabited, although a William Stoney leased it from the Marquis of Sligo in the mid-19th century.

Inishlaughil

Latitude: 53°51'37"N
Longitude: 9°37'59"W

Normal Grid Ref = L 925 913
10-digit Grid Ref = L 92560 91371

28 acres (25th largest island in Clew Bay)
Highest Point: 147 feet/45 metres (4th)

Inishlaughil Island (Inis Leamh Coill – Elm Wood Island) is an uninhabited island located in Newport Bay. It is situated north of Inishcottle and south of Inishfesh.

Inishloy

Latitude: 53°51'45"N
Longitude: 9°35'7"W

Normal Grid Ref = L 956 915
10-digit Grid Ref = L 95693 91542

21 acres (35th largest island in Clew Bay)
Highest Point: 105 feet/32 metres

Inishloy Island (Inis Laidhe – Island of the Spade) is an uninhabited island located in Newport Bay. It is situated west of Rossow Point, and east of Inishdaff. Unusually, a small house exists on the western (Atlantic-facing) side of the island.

Inishmolt

Latitude: 53°51'54"N
Longitude: 9°37'24"W

Normal Grid Ref = L 932 918
10-digit Grid Ref = L 93267 91873

4 acres (70th largest island in Clew Bay)
Highest Point: 56 feet/17 metres (64th)

Inishmolt Island (Inis Molt – Island of the Wethers) is a small uninhabited island located in Newport Bay. It is situated south of Inishcuill, and just east of Inishfesh. There is a building located near an extensive sand and shingle beach in the northeast corner of the island.

Inishturlin

Latitude: 53°52'34"N
Longitude: 9°36'4"W

Normal Grid Ref = L 947 930
10-digit Grid Ref = L 94762 93068

20 acres (37th largest island in Clew Bay)
Highest Point: 28 metres/94 feet (34th)

Inishturlin Island (Inis Dhuirlinge – Rounded Shore Island) is an uninhabited island situated in Newport Bay. It is situated west of the Knockeragh peninsula, which is located south of Newport harbour, and northwest of Rosbarnagh island. This island was included in what were known as the Tithe Applotment Books of the English Crown between 1823-1838. The tithe system, which nominally earmarked one-tenth of the produce of the land for the maintenance of the clergy, demanded cash from those who produced income from the land during this time. The books show that there were six individuals earning money from Inishturlin in 1832, with Hugh Purcell and Austin O'Malley having to pay four shillings and one pence each in tithes, while the remaining eight pounds and two pence were split evenly among the other lessees. In 1841, prior to the great famine, Inishturlin had twenty-five inhabitants. In 1851, that number had risen to thirty-six.

Muckinish

Latitude: 53°52'47"N
Longitude: 9°37'30"W

Normal Grid Ref = L 931 934
10-digit Grid Ref = L 93128 93477

25 acres (30th largest island in Clew Bay)
Highest Point: 120 feet/36 metres (13th)

Muckinish Island (Mucinis – Pig's Island) is an uninhabited island situated in Newport Bay. It is situated southwest of Inishdaweel and Rosmore Point. Unlike its neighbour Inishdaweel, Muckinish was not populated during the famine years.

Rabbit (Newport Bay)

Latitude: 53°52'46"N
Longitude: 9°35'48"W

Normal Grid Ref = L 950 934
10-digit Grid Ref = L 95019 93445

14 acres (49th largest island in Clew Bay)
Highest Point: 91 feet/28 metres (38th)

Rabbit Island (Oileán na gCoinín) is an uninhabited island in Newport Bay. It is situated on the south side of the mouth of the Newport Channel, just offshore from the Milcum peninsula and Rosnambraher Point.

NOTE - There are two Rabbit Islands in Clew Bay, the other being situated just north of Island More.

Rosbarnagh

Latitude: 53°52'20"N
Longitude: 9°35'31"W

Normal Grid Ref = L 952 925
10-digit Grid Ref = L 95281 92566

52 Acres (10th largest island on Clew Bay)
Highest Point: 129 feet/39 metres (9th)

Rosbarnagh (Ros Bairneach) is an uninhabited island in Newport Bay situated just north of the Rossanarubble peninsula and southeast of Inishturlin. It can be reached by following the N59 south of Newport for 1.5 kilometres, then taking a right at the signpost for Rossanarubble, staying right to see Rosbarnagh Island.

In 1841, the island had nine houses and forty-two residents, but this dwindled by half during the famine years, and no inhabitants by the late 19th century. There is a large house on this tree-lined island, which is reached from the mainland at low tide. The occupants of the house had originally built a causeway, but were ordered to remove it.

Roslynagh

Latitude: 53°53'17"N
Longitude: 9°37'2"W

Normal Grid Ref = L 935 943
10-digit Grid Ref = L 93510 94380

15 Acres (46th Largest island in Clew Bay)
Highest Point: 107 feet/31 metres (17th)

Roslynagh (Ros Laighneach – Limpet Headland) is an uninhabited island in Newport Bay, situated off the western tip of the Ardagh peninsula, east of Illanambraher. Twelve people lived on this island in three houses in

1841, but ten years later it was abandoned, and has not been inhabited since. The closest view may be obtained by turning left off the N59 onto an unmarked road just under five kilometres from Newport and keeping to the right while proceeding south. However, the headland at Ardagh is out of bounds on a private road.

Rosmore

Latitude: 53°53'12"N
Longitude: 9°34'45"W

Normal Grid Ref = L 964 942
10-digit Grid Ref = L 96443 94252

77 acres (5th Largest island in Clew Bay)
Highest Point: 92 feet/28 metres (37th)

Rosmore (An Ros Mor – Big Headland) is an inhabited island in Newport Bay, situated on the Newport Channel just north of the town – turn left at the Mulroy Motors sign about four kilometres out of town, on the N59. It is connected to the mainland via a bridge that is little more than twenty feet in length, making its case for being considered a true 'island' somewhat dubious.

In the early 1800's, there were ninety people living in thirteen houses on Rosmore, now there is a solitary farm in operation on the island. The headland provides a nice view of the islands clustered around the entrance to Newport Channel, including Inishdaweel, Muckinish, Freaghillanluggagh and Rabbit Island. Also, looking into the bay north of Rosmore, just east of the Burrishoole Channel, there is a cluster of small islands, including Illanavrick, Forillan, the impressive Camel Island, and the tongue-twisting rocks of Carrigeenaskibbole and Corragaunnagalliaghdoo.

Rosturk

Latitude: 53°53'11"N
Longitude: 9°39'58"W

Normal Grid Ref = L 914 945
10-digit Grid Ref = L 91464 94506

34 Acres (15th largest island in Clew Bay)
Highest Point: 106 feet/32 metres (19th)

Rosturk (Ros Toirc – Boar's Headland) is an uninhabited island situated in Newport Bay – to the west of Rockfleet Bay and at the tip of the Raigh peninsula. It is closest to Inishquirk island and the western part of Illannambraher island. It could be argued that Rosturk is really part of the mainland, since it is currently separated only by a thin strip of shingle. A lane seven kilometres past Newport on the N59 towards Mulranny leads part of the way down the peninsula towards Rosturk.

In 1841, there were 15 houses occupied by 64 people on Rosturk. It even had a coast guard station and a schoolhouse at one time. Twenty years later only one house remained, but there were no inhabitants left on the island. A family lived there in the early 20th century, but it is currently uninhabited.

Rosturk sits at the western end of Rockfleet Bay.

Northwest Clew Bay

Northwest Clew Bay includes the many small islands situated west of Newport closer to Mulranny.

- Beetle Island North
- Freaghillan West
- Illanoona
- Inishacrick
- Inishbobunnan
- Inishcannon
- Inishcooa
- Inishcorky
- Inishdasky
- Inishdeash More
- Inishdoonver
- Inisherkin
- Inishgowla (near Inishbobunnan)
- Inishgowla (near Inishoo)
- Inishilra
- Inishkeel
- Inishlim
- Inishnacross
- Inishoo
- Inishquirk
- Inishtubbrid
- Moynish More
- Roeillaun

NOTE - The islands of Northwest Clew Bay are best seen from side roads off the N59 road between Raigh (watch out for a sign for "Killeen Cemetery" on the main road) and Mulranny (sometimes spelled Mallaranny)

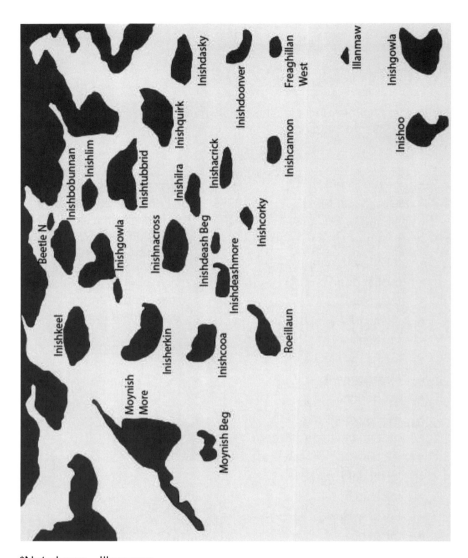

*Not shown - Illanoona

Beetle Island North

Latitude: 53°49'8"N
Longitude: 9°37'19"W

Normal Grid Ref = L 891 955
10-digit Grid Ref = L 89100 95545

2 acres (77th Largest Island in Clew Bay)

Beetle Island North (Oileán an tSindile Thuaidh) is a small uninhabited island situated just northeast of Inishbobunnan. The closest viewing point on the mainland is just off the N59 road towards Mulranny, about eleven kilometres west of Newport (left at St. Brendan's Church in Newfield).

The remains of a ring fort exist on Beetle Island North.

Freaghillan West

Latitude: 53°52'25"N
Longitude: 9°39'13"W

Normal Grid Ref = L 912 928
10-digit Grid Ref = L 91255 92844

3 acres (71st Largest Island in Clew Bay)
Highest Point: 62 feet/19 metres

Freaghillan West (Fraochoileán Thiar or Heather Island West) is an uninhabited island located just west of Inishkee and south of Inishdoonver. Its ownership was formerly attributed to Captain Hon. Windham Henry Wyndham-Quin (1829-1865).

Freaghillan West is difficult to spot from the mainland. It may be seen by looking west from the tip of Rosbarnagh Island.

Illanoona

Latitude: 53°54' N
Longitude: 9°46'W

2 acres (78th Largest Island in Clew Bay)
Highest Point: TBD

Normal Grid Ref = L 833 959
10-digit Grid Ref = L 83344 95939

Illanoona (Oileán Úna) is an uninhabited island situated on the shore opposite Mulranny Pier. It has been slowly eroding for years and little is left now. In 1855, it was leased by Captain Alexander Wyndham of Milcum for two pounds, two shilling and twenty-four pence. During the 1930's, the erosion led to the appearance of many bones of people thought to have been buried there during the famine years.

Inishacrick

Latitude: 53°52'44"N
Longitude: 9°40'34"W

Normal Grid Ref = L 897 934
10-digit Grid Ref = L 89745 93471

6 acres (62nd Largest Island in Clew Bay)
Highest Point: 76 feet/23 metres (51st)

Inishacrick (Inis an Chnoic – Island of the Hill) – sometimes named as "Inishcarrick" - is an uninhabited island situated southeast of Inishilra and north of Inishcannon.

Inishacrick is one of several small remote islands in the northwest area of the bay.

Inishbobunnan

Latitude: 53°53'46"N
Longitude: 9°41'19"W

Normal Grid Ref = L 888 954
10-digit Grid Ref = L 88857 95401

24 acres (32nd Largest Island in Clew Bay)
Highest Point: 102 feet/31 metres (25th)

Inishbobunnan (Inis Bó Bonnán – believed to be 'The Island of the Yellow Bittern') is an uninhabited island situated just offshore about 11 kilometres west of Newport, and north of Inishgowla island.

Inishcannon

Latitude: 53°52'25"N
Longitude: 9°40'22"W

Normal Grid Ref = L 899 928
10-digit Grid Ref = L 89957 92886

3 acres (74th largest island in Clew Bay)
Highest Point: 73 feet /22 metres (53rd)

Inishcannon Island (Inis Ceannann – Island of the Blaze) is a remote uninhabited island located south of Inishacrick and north of Inishoo Island. Like several of the more exposed islands in the northwest section of Clew Bay, Inishcannon has almost no vegetation. Its southern shore has been significantly eroded.

Inishcooa

Latitude: 53°52'54"N
Longitude: 9°42'32"W

Normal Grid Ref = L 876 938
10-digit Grid Ref = L 87622 93814

20 acres (36th largest island in Clew Bay)
Highest Point: 96 feet/29 metres (31st)

Inishcooa Island (Inis Cua – translation uncertain) is an uninhabited island located north of Roeillaun and south of Inisherkin. There is very little vegetation on this island, which unusually shows cliffs on the north side, rather than the west.

Inishcorky

Latitude: 53°52'35"N
Longitude: 9°41'8"W

Normal Grid Ref = L 891 932
10-digit Grid Ref = L 89163 93225

3 acres (75th largest island in Clew Bay)
Highest Point: 45 feet/14 metres (57th)

Inishcorky Island (Inis Corcaí- Cork Island) is a remote uninhabited island situated South of Inishdeashbeg and east of Roeillaun. This small island has an unusual ridge running through its middle, and unlike its neighbours has fairly lush vegetation.

Inishdasky

Latitude: 53°53'1"N
Longitude: 9°39'21"W

Normal Grid Ref = L 910 939
10-digit Grid Ref = L 91084 93960

15 acres (43rd Largest island in Clew Bay)
Highest Point: 100 feet/30 metres (27th)

Inishdasky Island (Inis Teasctha – Disc Island) is an uninhabited island located northwest of Newport Bay. It is situated just offshore, south of Rosturk and northwest of Inishcoragh. There is a summer house located in a sheltered spot with a path to a natural jetty at the northeast end of the island. There are also a significant number of lazybeds on the island.

Inishdeash More

Latitude: 53°52'45"N
Longitude: 9°41'49"W

Normal Grid Ref = L 883 935
10-digit Grid Ref = L 88369 93540

6 acres (63rd Largest island in Clew Bay)
Highest Point: 66 feet/20 metres (59th)

Inishdeash More Island (Inis Déise Mór – translation uncertain) is an uninhabited island located in Newport Bay. It is situated northeast of Roeillaun and east of Inishcooa. This fairly remote island boasts an unusual amount of agricultural activity, with extensive furrows crisscrossing every piece of land. There is also a long 'tail' of land at the eastern end.

Inishdoonver

Latitude: 53°52'39"N
Longitude: 9°39'12"W

Normal Grid Ref = L 912 932
10-digit Grid Ref = L 91225 93250

12 acres (51st Largest island in Clew Bay)
Highest Point: 88 feet/27 metres (30th)

Inishdoonver Island (Inis Dúnmhar – translation uncertain) is an uninhabited island located south of Inishdasky and north of Freaghillan West. This island shows extensive tilling, similar to Inishdeash More.

Inisherkin

Latitude: 53°53'18"N
Longitude: 9°42'16"W

Normal Grid Ref = L 877 944
10-digit Grid Ref = L 87711 94471

30 acres (19th largest island in Clew Bay)
Highest Point: 106 feet/32 metres (18th)

Inisherkin Island (Inis Earcain – translation uncertain) is an uninhabited island located in Newport Bay. This island includes the ruin of a once fine house and also a rampart.

Inishgowla

Latitude: 53°53'32"N
Longitude: 9°41'24"W

Normal Grid Ref = L 886 949
10-digit Grid Ref = L 88618 94965

31 acres (18th largest island in Clew Bay)
Highest Point: 111 feet/34 metres (15th)

One of two islands in Clew Bay named Inishgowla (Inis Gabhla – Fork Island), this fairly large uninhabited island is located close to the north shore just outside Newport Bay. In 1841, the island had twenty-eight people living on it (fourteen males and fourteen females), but ten years later, after the great famine, it was uninhabited.

Inishgowla

Latitude: 53°51'29"N
Longitude: 9°39'16"W

Normal Grid Ref = L 911 911
10-digit Grid Ref = L 91136 91117

32 acres (17th largest island in Clew Bay)
Highest Point: 96 feet/29 metres (32nd)

The 'other' Inishgowla Island (Inis Gabhla – Fork Island) is an uninhabited island located just east of Inishoo. In 1911, there were four houses on the island, with twenty-one occupants. The island itself is shaped somewhat like a horseshoe, complete with a small lake and a valley where the islanders used to live.

Inishilra

Latitude: 53°52'57"N
Longitude: 9°40'51"W

Normal Grid Ref = L 894 938
10-digit Grid Ref = L 89475 93872

8 acres (60th largest island in Clew Bay)
Highest Point: 66 feet/20 metres (60th)

Inishilra Island (Inis Iolra – translation uncertain) is an uninhabited island located south of Inishtubbrid and north of Inishacrick. The ruins of a house are located at the western end of the island. This house was inhabited by a family of twelve prior to the great famine.

Inishkeel

Latitude: 53°53'42"N
Longitude: 9°42'19"W

Normal Grid Ref = L 877 952
10-digit Grid Ref = L 87756 95290

30 acres (20th largest island in Clew Bay)
Highest Point: 90 feet/27 metres (40th)

Inishkeel Island (Inis Caol – Slender Island) is an uninhabited island located just offshore, northeast of Moynish More and west of Inishbobunnan. It is best seen from Rossgalliv Strand. The remains of a ring fort exist on the eastern side of the island. Twenty-three residents lived in three houses on Inishkeel prior to the great famine.

Inishlim

Latitude: 53°53'37"N
Longitude: 9°40'44"W

Normal Grid Ref = L 895 951
10-digit Grid Ref = L 89508 95124

6 acres (64th largest island in Clew Bay)
Highest Point: 88 feet/27 metres (41st)

Inishlim Island (Inis Loim – Milk Island) is an uninhabited island located north of Inishtubbrid and southeast of Inishbobunnan. There is a ring fort near the highest point on the island, although there are no records of it being inhabited.

Inishnacross

Latitude: 53°53'3"N
Longitude: 9°41'25"W

Normal Grid Ref = L 888 940
10-digit Grid Ref = L 88831 94087

25 acres (30th largest island in Clew Bay)
Highest Point: 123 feet/37 metres (11th)

Inishnacross Island (Inis na Croise – Island of the Cross) is an uninhabited island northwest of Newport. It is located south of Inishgowla and north of Inishdeash Beg. In 1841, twenty-seven people lived on Inishnacross. Not one remained after the famine, but the remains of their houses still exist on the island, which also has an artificial docking area on its eastern end.

Inishoo

Latitude: 53°51'18"N
Longitude: 9°40'16"W

Normal Grid Ref = L 901 911
10-digit Grid Ref = L 90154 91140

17 acres (41st Largest island in Clew Bay)
Highest Point: 104 feet/32 metres (27th)

Inishoo Island - formerly Inishue (Inis Umha – Island of the Cave) is an uninhabited island located north of Inishbee. Once the home of a coastguard station, this beautiful horseshoe-shaped island boasts a sandy swimming beach and a very high southwest-facing cliff that offers protection from the Atlantic gales.

Inishquirk

Latitude: 53°53'13"N
Longitude: 9°39'53"W

Normal Grid Ref = L 904 942
10-digit Grid Ref = L 90453 94274

28 acres (26th largest island in Clew Bay)
Highest Point: 144 feet/44 metres (6th)

Inishquirk Island (Inis Coirce – Island of the Oats) is an uninhabited island located just off the Roskeen peninsula. It is southeast of Inishtubbrid and northwest of Inishdasky. In 1841, thirty-seven people lived in Inishquirk. Seventeen remained ten years later.

Annagh Islands

Latitude: 53°47'27"N
Longitude: 9°35'36"W

Normal Grid Ref = L 953 834
10-digit Grid Ref = L 95343 83451

Annagh East
47 acres (12th Largest Island in Clew Bay). Highest Point: 30 feet (73rd highest)

Annagh Middle
11 acres (54th Largest Island in Clew Bay). Highest Point: 11 feet (76th highest)

Annagh West
17 acres (40th Largest Island in Clew Bay). Highest Point: 34 feet (72nd highest)

Annagh (Oileán an Eanaigh – Marsh Island) is an uninhabited group of three islands situated in Westport Bay, just east of Murrisk. The islands are named Annagh West, Annagh Middle and Annagh East. These are located just off the Murrisk road, about nine kilometres from Westport.

In 1841, Annagh East was inhabited by 33 people. After the famine, no one remained. Little trace of any dwelling remains today. Annagh is protected from the open ocean by the Murrisk headland and the dunes and shingle of Bartraw.

Bartraw

Latitude: 53°47'55"N
Longitude: 9°39'2"W

Normal Grid Ref = L 912 844
10-digit Grid Ref = L 91235 84442

25 acres (28th Largest island in Clew Bay).
Highest point: 147 feet (5th highest)

As it is still attached to the mainland by means of a long bar of shingle and sand dunes, Bartraw (sometimes locally pronounced 'Berthroy' – Bar Strand) is not technically an island, but a 'semi island' located at the end of a sand and shingle bar in Westport Bay. This is a rare example of a 'tombolo' - a deposition landform in which an island is attached to the mainland by a narrow piece of land such as a spit or bar. It is a very popular beach destination about 12 kilometres west of Westport, just beyond Murrisk.

In 1889, a thirty-year old local man named John Hanlon was drowned in the narrow but deep channel that runs between Bartraw and the island of Inishdaugh (sometimes referred to as 'Inistraugh' and phonetically as 'Inish Chalk'). Apparently, Hanlon and three other men had used their horses to cross the channel to the island to gather seaweed, but had spent a lot of time examining a schooner that was moored nearby. A squall caught them by surprise, and the high waves and strong current as the tide turned swept Hanlon off his horse. His body was later found on the other side of Inishdaugh.

According to local legend, earlier in the day Hanlon had teased a solitary man who used to gather seaweed at Bartraw by scattering his 'wrack' of weed around the shore. The man had told anyone he met that day that he was praying the one who did it would be soon dead and buried.

Cahernaran Island

Latitude: 53°47'18"N
Longitude: 9°38'32"W

Normal Grid Ref = L 918 832
10-digit Grid Ref = L 91858 83248

4 acres (67th Largest Island in Clew Bay)
Highest Point: 30 feet (75th Highest)

Cahernaran Island (Oileán Chathair na Reann – Island of the City of Rann) is an uninhabited island situated in Westport Bay, south of Inisheeny. It is located just off the R335 road towards Louisburgh, on the right just before the Great Famine monument in Murrisk, about nine kilometres west of Westport (right at Carrowsallagh). It is easily accessible at low tide.

Cahernaran was known for an ancient stone fort, now destroyed. It is believed that a local chieftain named Rann once lived there.

Crovinish

Latitude: 53°49'2"N
Longitude: 9°38'29"W

Normal Grid Ref = L 918 865
10-digit Grid Ref = L 91879 86583

28 acres (22nd Largest Island in Clew Bay)
Highest Point: 81 feet (48th Highest)

Crovinish (Croibhinis – formerly Creamh Inis or Garlic Island) is an uninhabited island situated in Westport Bay, southeast of Inishlyre and northwest of Inishgowla South. In 1841, the island had twenty-two inhabitants, and by 1911 there were still sixteen people living on the island in three thatched dwellings, each of which had two rooms. Sixty-year-old Martin Fadden and his thirty-nine-year-old wife Mary lived in one home with their eight children at that time.

Dorinish

Latitude: 53°50'49"N
Longitude: 9°38'27"W

Normal Grid Ref = L 899 860
10-digit Grid Ref = L 89955 86058

Dorinish More
9 acres (56th Largest Island in Clew Bay). Highest Point: 98 feet (29th Highest)

Dorinish Beg
5 acres (65th Largest Island in Clew Bay). Highest Point: 63 feet (63rd Highest)

Dorinish (Deoirinis – possibly Teardrop Island) More and Dorinish Beg are two uninhabited islands joined by a natural causeway situated at the mouth of Westport Bay, south of the lighthouse at Inishgort and northeast of Bartraw. Interestingly, the population of Dorinish actually grew from thirteen to seventeen before and after the famine years. These inhabitants lived in two houses.

Dorinish is perhaps the most famous of the inner Clew Bay islands due to its association with John Lennon of the Beatles, who bought it in 1967. Lennon never lived on the island, but allowed Sid Rawle, the "King of the Hippies" to establish a commune there for two years. After John's death, it was sold by Yoko Ono, who gave the money to a children's hospital.

The island of Dorinish More or 'Big Dorinish' boasts a huge clay cliff as it faces the outer bay without any protection from the Atlantic waves. It is separated from its smaller neighbour Dorinish Beg or 'Little Dorinish' by a strip of shingle. Dorinish's distinctive shape with its prominent spit to the northeast – at low tide being somewhat similar to a bird's outstretched wings - is best seen from the lower slopes of Croagh Patrick on a clear day, looking north across the bay. There are also the remnants of three small farms on the northeast side.

Illanataggart

Latitude: 53°49'10"N
Longitude: 9°37'39"W

Normal Grid Ref = L 928 867
10-digit Grid Ref = L 92822 86781

29 acres (22nd Largest Island in Clew Bay)
Highest Point: 87 feet (43rd)

Illanataggart (Oileán an tSagairt – Priest's Island) is an uninhabited island in Newport Bay, situated between Crovinish Island and the Rosmoney Peninsula. In 1841, there were 33 persons living on this island and by 1911 just seven resided there in two houses. There is a holiday home on the island today.

Illanroe

Latitude: 53°47'43"N
Longitude: 9°34'30"W

Normal Grid Ref = L 963 840
10-digit Grid Ref = L 96307 84039

4 acres (79th Largest Island in Clew Bay).
Highest Point: 43 feet (70th)

Illanroe (Oileán Rua – Red Island) is an uninhabited island situated in Westport Bay, east of the tip of Annagh Island and near the village of Rosbeg (about five kilometres west of Westport town centre).

Inishdaugh

Latitude: 53°48'8"N
Longitude: 9°38'51"W

Normal Grid Ref = L 912 844
10-digit Grid Ref = L 91241 84447

6 acres (62nd Largest island in Clew Bay)
Highest Point: 75 feet (52nd)

Inishdaugh Island (Inis Deách – translation uncertain) is an uninhabited island located in Westport Bay, just off the tip of Bartraw. The tidal race between Bartraw and Inishdaugh is very strong and this narrow channel is deep. It is often used by boats bound for Westport Quay.

Local tradition claims that Inishdaugh is the richest island in the bay. Legend has it that the Danes buried a pile of gold on the island and that every seven years a cave appears to provide access to this treasure. The guardian of the treasure must be felled by a silver two-shilling piece with a cross on it. The story goes on to claim that a Norwegian sea captain attempted to find this treasure by employing local men to dig on the island, but was unsuccessful.

Inisheeny

Latitude: 53°50'49"N
Longitude: 9°38'27"W

Normal Grid Ref = L 920 845
10-digit Grid Ref = L 92035 84536

25 acres (29th Largest Island in Clew Bay)
Highest Point: 72 feet (54th)

Inisheeny (Inis Aonaigh – Market Island) is an uninhabited island located in Westport Bay. In the years before and after the great famine, however, this island, which lies close to the Murrisk shore, was highly populated. By 1911, there were three two-room houses on the island inhabited by sixteen members of the Grady and Kelly families.

Inishgowla South

Latitude: 53°48'40"N
Longitude: 9°37'53"W

Normal Grid Ref = L 926 858
10-digit Grid Ref = L 92648 85831

28 acres (24th largest island in Clew Bay)
Highest Point: 64 feet (62nd)

Inishgowla South Island (Inis Gabhla Theas – South Island of the Fork) is an uninhabited island located in Westport Bay. A self-catering rental cottage now stands on the north, shallower side of the island.

Inishimmel

Latitude: 53°48'33"N
Longitude: 9°39'29"W

Normal Grid Ref = L 907 856
10-digit Grid Ref = L 90789 85688

3 acres (76th largest island in Clew Bay)
Highest Point: 51 feet (66th)

Inishimmel Island (Inis Imill – Cropped Island) is a small uninhabited island located in Westport Bay. It is situated east of Dorinish Beg and north of Inishleague.

Inishleague

Latitude: 53°48'19"N
Longitude: 9°39'18"W

Normal Grid Ref = L 909 852
10-digit Grid Ref = L 90960 85250

13 acres (50th largest island in Clew Bay)
Highest Point: 27 metres / 86 feet (44th)

Inishleague Island (Inis Liag – Stone Island) is an uninhabited island located in Westport Bay. The remnants of a house exist at the northern edge of the island, as well as evidence of potato furrows. There are high cliffs on the southern edges.

Inishlyre

Latitude: 53°49'24"N
Longitude: 9°39'5"W

Normal Grid Ref = L 911 872
10-digit Grid Ref = L 91181 87225

52 acres (9th largest island in Clew Bay)
Highest Point: 104 feet (21st)

Inishlyre Island (Inis Ladhair – some translate this as 'Harp Island') is an inhabited island located in Westport Bay. Currently, there are two permanent and two holiday homes in the natural harbour on the east side of the island. Several shipwrecks have occurred in this area (see 'The Wrecks of Clew Bay'). The two-mile journey from Rosmoney Harbour to the island may take half an hour by boat. There were two pubs and a hotel on the island in the 19th century. Some residents were known to row children to school on the nearby island of Collan More.

Merchants dropped cargo on Inishlyre because there was no deep-sea harbour in Westport. The islanders then shipped the goods to the mainland in smaller boats. Even American Liners were able to moor in the deep harbour of Inishlyre. The government even proposed making Inishlyre a port-of-call for ocean-going ships. This met with little enthusiasm from the county council and Midland Great Western Railway, who refused to build a connecting railway to Westport. In 1841, before the Famine, the island had a population of 113. At last count (in 2011) there were four people living on the island.

Inishraher

Latitude: 53°48'18"N
Longitude: 9°37'52"W

Normal Grid Ref = L 925 851
10-digit Grid Ref = L 92531 85174

26 acres (27th largest island in Clew Bay)
Highest Point: 104 feet (23rd)

Inishraher (Inis Raithneach – Island of the Ferns) is an inhabited island located in Westport Bay, south of Inishgowla South and northeast of Inisheeny.

A cluster of houses and other buildings sit at the eastern end of the island. It is believed that Inishraher is currently occupied all year round by members of the TM organization, who offer retreats during the summer and autumn months.

In 1911, there were two houses on Inishraher, each with two rooms, occupied by eight people ranging in age from sixteen to seventy-four from the Joyce and Jordan families.

In 2005, Inishraher was named as a Maharishi Capital of the Global Country of World Peace.

Roman Island

Latitude: 53°48'6"N
Longitude: 9°33'23"W

Normal Grid Ref = L 974 847
10-digit Grid Ref = L 97470 84707

8 acres (68th largest island in Clew Bay)
Highest Point: 45 feet (69th)

Roman Island (Oileán na Rómhánach) is situated at the western end of Westport Quay. Known locally as 'The Point', the Westport Heritage Centre and the Westport Sailing Club are both located here. It is also the former home of the Bath Hotel. Birdwatchers often come here hoping to catch sight of Mergansers, Mute Swans, Grebes, Kingfishers and Divers. The western end of Roman Island is said to be mainly comprised of buried ships ballast.

Westport Quay itself, which runs the length of the northern side of Roman Island, was established in 1780 and extended in 1837. At its commercial peak, the quay was home to a herring fishing fleet.

In 1894, a tragedy occurred near Roman Island when a hooker carrying passengers from Achill Island overturned and thirty-five people drowned. The passengers, who had paid sixpence each for the trip from Achill were mainly young people bound for the harvest fields of Scotland on the steamer S.S. Elm. The passengers had all moved to one side of the boat Clare Island sits at the entrance to Clew Bay. It is the best known and most recognisable of all the islands, with its peak of Knockmore (462 metres) and colourful history. The other islands in this section lie outside Clew Bay, but are significant enough to be easily seen from Croagh Patrick on a fine day.

Clare Island and the Outlying Islands

- Achillbeg
- Caher Island
- Clare Island
- Inishbofin
- Inishshark
- Inishturk

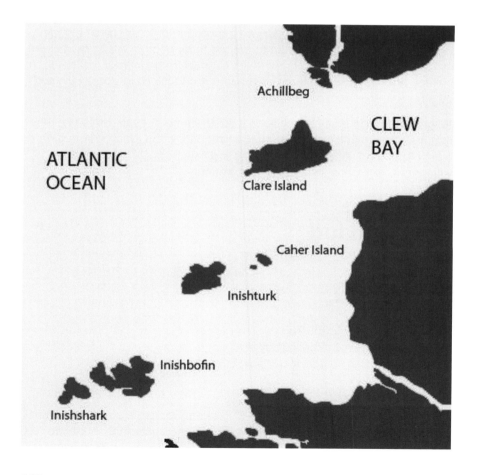

Achillbeg

Latitude: 53°86.61'N
Longitude: 9°95.01'W

Normal Grid Ref = L 717 925
10-digit Grid Ref = L 71730 92506

330 acres
Highest Point: 110 metres/360 feet

Achillbeg (Little Achill) is a relatively large uninhabited island on the northern fringes of Clew Bay. was once home to a large community of islanders. These numbered over two hundred prior to the great famine. By the 1960s this had dwindled to around thirty people. It was evacuated in 1965 and has been empty ever since, apart from summer visitors to holiday homes. The island is separated from Achill, its larger neighbour, by a narrow channel called the Blind Sound.

A lighthouse was built on Achillbeg's southern tip in 1965, the same year that the remaining inhabitants left the island for good, despite retaining most of the land. Access to the island today is from *Cé Mhór*, in the village of Cloghmore, by local arrangement.

Caher Island

Latitude: 53°43.3'N
Longitude: 10°1.48'W

Normal Grid Ref = L 659 760
10-digit Grid Ref = L 65927 76069

128 acres
Highest Point: 61 metres/201 feet

Caher Island (Cathair na Naomh – City of the Saints) is a remote, almost inaccessible island that lies in the North Atlantic east of the inhabited island of Inishturk, and south of Clare Island. This island is significant to

Christian pilgrims as it is believed that Saint Patrick once landed there. An early Christian monastery with the remains of the original 7th century carved crosses still exists on the island. The Island is also believed to have contained the hermitage sites of seventh century monks. Caher is associated with High Island (south of Inishshark) and also to Inishmurray in Sligo. These were outposts of early Christian settlements. For example, a wall chamber on Caher is similar to one on Inishmurray, and may have been used by solitary religious people known as "anchorites".

Once a year, on August 15th, the Christian Feast of the Assumption, a pilgrims' boat leaves Inishturk with the intention of landing on Caher. This is not always possible due to the heavy sea swells around this rugged place. Caher can only be accessed reasonably safely by approaching with a small boat, such as a currach, from the east to the point marked as Portatemple, which is located at the southeast end of the island.

The island has a small church and a holy well. One of the archaeological highlights is a cross slab, about 30 inches high, embossed with a large Greek cross above two dolphins. A medieval pilgrimage route was discovered on the island in 2014. Archaeologists believe that the discovery of the pilgrimage "round," or circuit on the island helped to explain a 1,000-year-old religious ritual that involved a trek to the top of Croagh Patrick along the Tochar Padraig, then following *Bóthair na Naomh* (the Saints Road) to its sea end at Caher Island. The larger pilgrimage arc on the south and west sides of the island includes several 'leachts' or altars. These have not been maintained since the island was abandoned in 1838. It is believed that there are many unmapped archaeological treasures yet to be discovered on Caher.

Clare Island

Latitude: 53°48.13′N
Longitude: 9°59.32′W

Normal Grid Ref = L 686 856
10-digit Grid Ref = L 68667 85642

3949 acres (Largest Island in Clew Bay)
Highest Point: 462 metres/1516 feet (Highest point in the bay)

Clare Island (Oileán Chliara) guards the entrance to Clew Bay, and is easily visible from all parts of the bay. At almost 4,000 acres and with over twenty kilometres of coastline, it is twice as large as all of the other islands in the bay combined. Its highest point – Knockmore (1516 feet) - is also more than seven times higher than the next highest point in the bay (on Collan More at 199 feet). At the time of writing, Clare Island also had almost six times as many inhabitants (145) than all of the other islands combined. However, this is a big decrease from the pre-famine years in the 1800's, when the island had over 1,500 residents.

Knox, in his 'History of County Mayo', reported that "the most picturesque run (to Clare Island) is from Westport down the most charming bay on the coast. Thus only can you realise what Clew Bay, with its 365 isles, is like".

Clare Island is the only one of the Clew Bay islands with a regular year-round ferry service from the mainland. In fact, there are two ferry services that carry passengers across the five kilometres from Roonagh Quay to the island. One of these companies is run by the O'Malley family, who are descendants of the legendary 'Pirate Queen' Grace O'Malley, otherwise known as Gráinne Mhaol (anglicised as Granuaile).

Grace O'Malley spent her childhood on Clare Island during the 16th century (the O'Malleys built several castles in the Clew Bay area, including the one that stands today on the shores of Clare Island. It was from here and other areas of Clew Bay that she later conducted a lucrative shipping and trading business (referred to as piracy by her enemies) from her father. She was a native Gaelic speaker, well-educated and by all accounts a formidable businesswoman. Most famously, she went to London to petition Elizabeth I for the release of her sons and half-brother and refused to bow before the Queen, whom she did not recognize as the ruler of Ireland at the time. It is believed that they spoke in Latin at their meeting.

In the 19th century, the inhabitants of Clare Island unsuccessfully attempted to set up an independent principality or 'kingdom', and even nominated a 'king' of the island. However, their English rulers continued to subject them to county rates, "little of which they pay", according to the Parliamentary Gazetteer.

William Thackeray wrote that "in the centre of the bay is Clare Island, of which the edges were bright with cobalt, whilst the middle was lighted up with a brilliant scarlet tinge, such as I would have laughed at in a picture, never having seen it in nature before, but looked at it now with wonder and pleasure".

Today, Clare Island is a popular destination for visitors to the Westport area, with its ample accommodations and stunning scenery. The old lighthouse on the edge of the Atlantic still survives, although it is now a guest house.

About twelve kilometres WNW of Clare Island lie Bills Rocks. These rocks tower up to forty metres above the waves, and are at least as deep beneath the Atlantic. This remote location was used as a firing range up to the end of World War I, and the remnants of shell casings can still be found there.

Kinatevdilla is found at the western point of Clare island. It is a derivation of Ceann-a-tseimhdile, or Beetle Head.

Inishbofin

Latitude: 53°37.13′N
Longitude: 10°12.41′W

Normal Grid Ref = L 536 656
10-digit Grid Ref = L 53696 65674

3401 acres
Highest Point: 89 metres/292 feet

Inishbofin (Inis Bo Finne - Island of the White Cow) is an island located in the North Atlantic off the Connemara coast, south of Inishturk. As with Inishturk, this is a large island that can be seen from Croagh Patrick on a clear day.

It is believed that Inishbofin may have been inhabited as long ago as the Iron Age. Around 665, Saint Colmán founded a Christian monastery on the island. According to local tradition, in the 16th century a Spanish pirate built a stronghold on Inishbofin, where a Cromwellian fort that was later built to imprison catholic priests still stands today. According to the tales the Spaniard raided the Irish coast and shipping in the area. "Don" Bosco was supposed to have been an ally of Grainne Uaile – 'The Pirate Queen'.

At one point in the early 19th century, Inishbofin belonged to the Browne family of Westport. By the end of that century, it was no longer a part of the barony of Murrisk and had legally switched from County Mayo to County Galway.

The island's population peaked at 1,404 just prior to the great famine. Today, there are still over one hundred and fifty residents and it is a popular tourist destination, known for its traditional music and outdoor activities.

Inishbofin can be reached by ferry from Cleggan in Connemara. There is also a helipad, and an airstrip has been built on the island.

Inishshark

Latitude: 53°36.39'N
Longitude: 10°16.52'W

Normal Grid Ref = L 490 647
10-digit Grid Ref = L 49052 64755

631 acres
Highest Point: 69 metres/227 feet

Inishshark (Inis Airc - Island of the Shark) is an uninhabited island lying
in the North Atlantic just southwest of Inishbofin. At one point in the 19th
century, there were over two hundred residents on the island, but in
1960, after the remaining twenty-three inhabitants had been isolated for
weeks due to bad winter storms, the government decided to relocate
them rather than build an expensive pier. Despite its proximity to
Inishbofin, a 19th century parish priest's assessment of Inishshark was
that "even a crow could not land on it when it is blowing and a heavy sea
running."

Inishturk

Latitude: 52°42.6'N
Longitude: 10°6.55'W

Normal Grid Ref = L 603 745
10-digit Grid Ref = L 60325 74535

Highest Point: 192 metres/629 feet

Inishturk (Inis Toirc - Wild Boar Island) is an inhabited island in the North
Atlantic, south of Clare Island. It can be reached by ferry from Roonagh
Quay on the mainland. It is considered one of the most beautiful of the
Irish islands.

It is believed than Inishturk was used by the Norsemen during their raids and that gold was found there. This is consistent with evidence of a gold seam that is said to run from Croagh Patrick to Inishturk.

The current Graveyard on Inishturk was on the site of a stone circle, indicating its pagan origins. The signal tower, almost two hundred metres above the waves, was built around 1805 by local labour. A number of Beehive house sites around the lake area were dated back to 1500 b.c.

Legend has it that a pirate crew on Inishturk were reputedly the last Danes in Ireland who knew how to make "bier lochlannach", a drink made from the heather-bloom. They were taken by the Irish who slaughtered everyone except for one old Dane and his son, offering to spare the captives if they told the secret of the bier, or the hiding place of their vast treasures, some of which are said to have been buried on Inishdaugh island in Westport Bay. The old pirate, fearing the boy might be tempted or tortured into betrayal offered to tell if his son was put to death first, so none of his kin might see his treachery. This done, the pirate captain tore himself from his captors and jumped into a deep chasm.

The population of Inishturk was decimated by the great famine. In 1841, there were 577 people living on the island. Ten years later, only 174 people remained. At the time of the last census, there were fifty-three people resident.

Ranking by Island Size

Rank	Island	Acres
1	Clare Island	3949
2	Collan More	199
3	Clynish	80
4	Island More	77
5	Rosmore	77
6	Moynish More	61
7	Inishturk Beg	59
8	Inishnakillew	58
9	Inishlyre	52
10	Rosbarnagh	52
11	Inishbee	51
12	Annagh East	47
13	Inishtubbrid	37
14	Knockycahillaun	34
15	Rosturk	34
16	Inishdaff	32
17	Inishgowla (Westport)	32
18	Inishgowla (Newport)	31
19	Inisherkin	30
20	Inishkeel	30
21	Derrinish	29
22	Illanataggart	29
23	Crovinish	28
24	Inishgowla South	28
25	Inishlaughil	28
26	Inishquirk	28
27	Inishraher	26
28	Bartraw	25
29	Inisheeny	25
30	Inishnacross	25
31	Muckinish	25
32	Inishbobunnan	24
33	Inishcottle	23
34	Inishgort	21
35	Inishloy	21
36	Inishcooa	20
37	Inishturlin	20
38	Rabbit Island (Westport)	20
39	Freaghillan	19
40	Annagh West	17
41	Inishoo	17
42	Collan Beg	16
43	Inishdasky	15
44	Inishdaweel	15
45	Roeillaun	15
46	Roslynagh	15
47	Illannambraher East	14
48	Inishcuill	14
49	Rabbit Island (Newport)	14
50	Inishleague	13
51	Inishdoonver	12
52	Inishfesh	12
53	Inishkee	12
54	Annagh Middle	11
55	Illannambraher West	11
56	Dorinish More	9
57	Moneybeg	9
58	Calf Island	8
59	Inishcoragh	8
60	Inishilra	8
61	Roman Island	8
62	Inishdaugh	6
63	Inishdeash More	6
64	Inishlim	6
65	Dorinish Beg	5
66	Inishacrick	5
67	Cahernaran	4
68	Illannaconney	4
69	Illaunnamona	4
70	Inishmolt	4
71	Freaghillan West	3
72	Freaghillanluggagh	3
73	Inishbollog	3
74	Inishcannon	3
75	Inishcorky	3
76	Inishimmel	3
77	Beetle Island North	2
78	Illanoona	2
79	Illanroe	2
80	Inishcuill West	2
81	Quinsheen	2

Ranking by Elevation above Sea Level

Rank	Island	Feet
1	Clare Island	1516
2	Collan More	174
3	Inishturk Beg	173
4	Inishlaughil	147
5	Bartraw	147
6	Inishquirk	144
7	Clynish	138
8	Rosbarnagh	129
9	Inishdaweel	128
10	Inishnacross	123
11	Moynish More	121
12	Muckinish	120
13	Knockycahillaun	119
14	Inishgowla (Newport)	111
15	Roeillaun	107
16	Roslynagh	107
17	Inisherkin	106
18	Rosturk	106
19	Inishgort	105
20	Inishlyre	104
21	Inishoo	104
22	Inishraher	104
23	Inishbee	102
24	Inishbobunnan	102
25	Inishdaff	101
26	Inishdasky	100
27	Beetle Island North	100
28	Dorinish More	98
29	Inishdoonver	98
30	Inishcooa	96
31	Inishgowla (Westport)	96
32	Inishnakillew	96
33	Inishturlin	94
34	Inishcuill	93
35	Inishtubbrid	92
36	Rosmore	92
37	Rabbit Island (Newport)	91
38	Inishcottle	90
39	Inishkeel	90
40	Inishlim	88
41	Freaghillan	87
42	Illanataggart	87
43	Inishleague	86
44	Collan Beg	83
45	Illannambraher East	83
46	Illannambraher West	82
47	Crovinish	81
48	Inishcoragh	79
49	Calf Island	76
50	Inishacrick	76
51	Inishdaugh	75
52	Inishcannon	73
53	Inisheeny	72
54	Derrinish	72
55	Island More	72
56	Rabbit Island (Westport)	72
57	Inishbollog	66
58	Inishdeash More	66
59	Inishilra	66
60	Freaghillanluggagh	65
61	Inishgowla South	64
62	Dorinish Beg	63
63	Inishmolt	63
64	Moneybeg	56
65	Inishimmel	51
66	Illannaconney	46
67	Inishkee	46
68	Roman Island	45
69	Inishcorky	45
70	Illanroe	43
71	Illaunnamona	36
72	Annagh West	34
73	Annagh East	30
74	Quinsheen	30
75	Cahernaran	30
76	Annagh Middle	11
	Freaghillan West	TBD
	Illanoona	TBD
	Inishcuill West	TBD
	Inishfesh	TBD
	Inishloy	TBD

Suggested Irish Language Names*

Island	Irish	Translation
Annagh East	An tEanach Thoir	East Marsh Island
Annagh Middle	An tEanach Lair	Middle Marsh Island
Annagh West	An tEanach Thiar	West Marsh Island
Bartraw	An Bheartrach	The Bar Strand
Beetle Island North	Oilean an tSindile Thuaidh	North Island of the Beetle
Calf Island	Oilean na nGeamhna	Island of the Calves
Clynish	Claidhnis	Island of the Ditch
Collan Beg	Cuileann Bheag	Little Holly
Collan More	Cuileann Mhor	Big Holly
Crovinish	Creamh Inis	Garlic Island
Derrinish	Doire Inis	Oakwood Island
Dorinish Beg	Deoirinis Bheag	Big Tear Island
Dorinish More	Deoirinis Mhor	Small Tear Island
Freaghillan West	Fraochoilean Thiar	Heather Island West
Freaghillanluggagh	Fraochoilean Logach	Hollow of the Heather Island
Freaghillan	Fraochoilean	Heather Island
Illanataggart	Oilean an tSagairt	Priest's Island
Illannambraher East	Oilean na mBrathar Thoir	East Island of the Brethren
Illannambraher West	Oilean na mBrathar Thiar	West Island of the Brethren
Illanroe	An tOilean Rua	The Red Island
Illanaconney	Oilean an Chonnaidh	Firewood Island
Illaunamona	Oilean na Mona	Turf Island
Inishacrick	Inis an Chnoic	Hill Island
Inishbee	Inish Buidhe	Yellow Island
Inishbobunnan	Inis Bo Bonnan	Yellow Bittern Island

These are suggested Irish translations only. Some of the spellings of the Clew Bay islands have changed over the years, and as such it is difficult to pinpoint exactly what the original name might have meant in English.

Suggested Irish Language Names (continued)

Island	Irish	Translation
Inishbollog	Inis Bolg	Stomach Island
Inishcannon	Inis Ceannann	Island of the Blaze
Inishcoragh	Inis Córach	Pleasant Island
Inishcorky	Inis Corcaí	Cork Island
Inishcottle	Inis Cotail	Cottle's Island
Inishcuill	Inis Coill	Wood Island
Inishcuill West	Inis Coill Thiar	Wood Island West
Inishdaff	Inis Damh	Ox Island
Inishdasky	Inis Teasctha	Disc Island
Inishdaweel	Inis Dá Mhaol	Island of Two Hornless Cows
Inisheeny	Inis Aonaigh	Market Island
Inishfesh	Inis Feise	Festival Island
Inishgort	Inis Goirt	Field Island
Inishgowla (Newport)	Inis Gabhla	Fork Island
Inishgowla (Westport)	Inis Gabhla	Fork Island
Inishgowla South	Inis Gabhla Theas	Fork Island South
Inishimmel	Inis Imill	Cropped Island
Inishkeel	Inis Caol	Slender Island
Inishlaughil	Inis Leamhchoille	Elmwood Island
Inishleague	Inis Liag	Stone Island
Inishlim	Inis Loim	Milk Island
Inishloy	Inis Láidhe	Island of the Spade
Inishlyre	Inis Ladhair	Fork Island
Inishmolt	Inis Molt	Island of the Wethers
Inishnacross	Inis na Croise	Island of the Cross

Suggested Irish Language Names (continued)

Island	Irish	Translation
Inishnakillew	Inis na Coilleadh	Island of the Wood
Inishoo	Inis Uamha	Island of the Cave
Inishquirk	Inis Coirce	Island of the Oats
Inishraher	Inis Raithir	Island of the Ferns
Inishtubbrid	Inis Tiobrad	Island of the Well
Inishturk Beg	Inis Toirc Beag	Small Boar Island
Inishturlin	Inis Dhuirlinge	Rounded Shore Island
Island More	an tOileán Mór	Big Island
Knockycahillaun	Cnoc Uí Chathaláin	Cahillaun's Island
Moneybeg	An Muine Beag	The small thicket
Muckinish	Mucinis	Pig's Island
Quinsheen	Cuinsín	Little Snub Nose
Rabbit Island (Westport)	Oileán na gCoinín	Rabbit Island
Rabbit Island (Newport)	Oileán na gCoinín	Rabbit Island
Roeillaun	Rua-oileán	Red Island
Roman Island	Oileán na Rómhánach	Roman Island
Roslynagh	Ros Laighneach	Limpet Headland
Rosmore	An Ros Mór	Big Headland
Rosturk	Ros Toirc	Boar's Headland

Island Population 1841 – 2011*

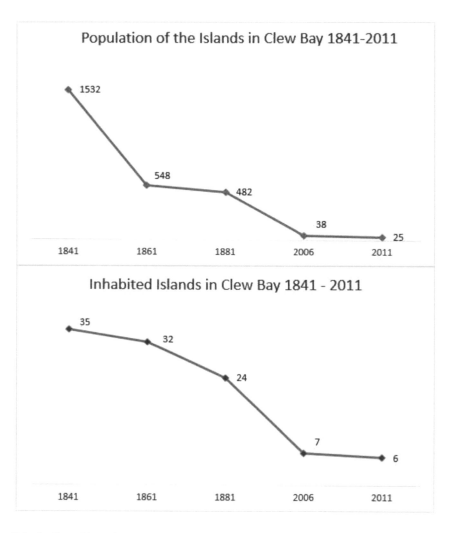

*Excluding Clare Island

Island Population 1841 – 2011 (continued)

Census Year	1841	1861	1881	2006	2011
Total Population	1532	548	482	38	25
Inhabited Islands	35	32	24	7	6

Island/Census Year	1841	1861	1881	2006	2011
Collan More	213	63	59	18	4
Inishnakillew	126	39	41	3	7
Inishlyre	113	61	67	7	4
Moynish More	99	6	4	0	0
Rosmore	9	8	0	0	0
Island More	88	45	21	1	0
Clynish	87	24	17	5	4
Rosturk	64	0	0	0	0
Inishturk Beg	57	2	2	0	1
Inishgowla (Westport)	53	4	43	0	0
Inishdaff	44	14	0	0	0
Inishtubbrid	42	29	27	0	0
Rosbarnagh	42	0	0	0	0
Knockycahillaun	41	37	18	0	0
Derrinish	4	16	9	0	0
Inishcottle	4	38	29	3	5
Inishquirk	37	3	5	0	0
Inisheeny	36	0	0	0	0
Annagh East	33	0	0	0	0
Illanataggart	33	25	24	0	0
Crovinish	32	3	21	0	0
Inishgort	32	3	23	1	0
Inishoo	29	1	4	0	0

*Excluding Clare Island

Island Population 1841 – 2011 (continued)

Island/Census Year	1841	1861	1881	2006	2011
Inisherkin	28	7	7	0	0
Inishgowla (Newport)	28	12	0	0	0
Inishnacross	27	6	0	0	0
Inishraher	25	3	21	0	0
Inishturlin	25	2	0	0	0
Inishkeel	23	0	0	0	0
Inishbee	2	11	13	0	0
Dorinish More	13	0	14	0	0
Inishbobunnan	13	15	0	0	0
Inishilra	12	0	0	0	0
Roslynagh	12	0	0	0	0
Inishcooa	6	9	0	0	0
Inishcuill	0	0	6	0	0
Inishfesh	0	1	3	0	0
Inishgowla South	0	39	0	0	0
Inishlim	0	6	0	0	0
Calf Island	0	7	0	0	0
Collan Beg	0	9	4	0	0

*Clare Island had a peak population of 1,615 in 1841, just before the famine years. By 1901, just 457 people occupied the island. In 2011, the population was 168.

Islands by Relative Position – Northern

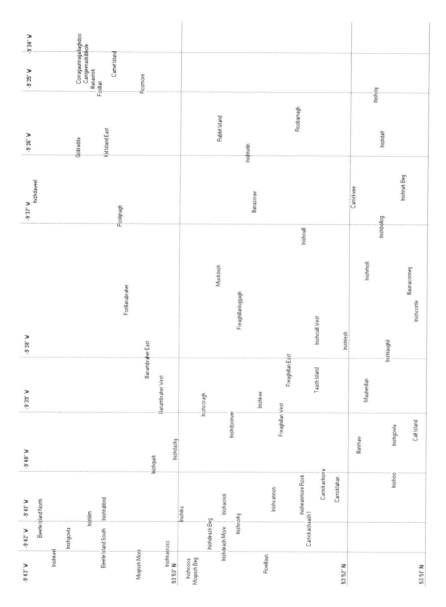

Islands by Relative Position – Southern

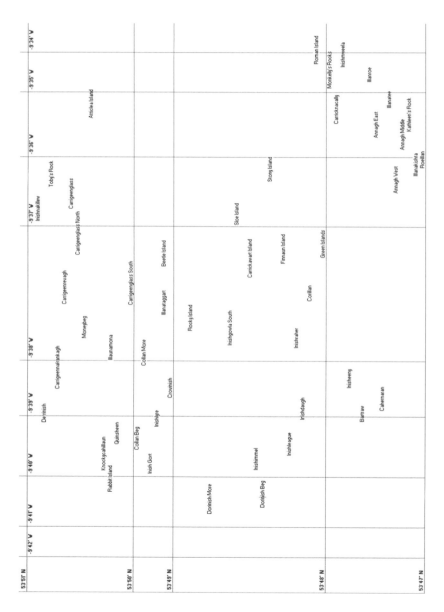

References

Burke's Peerage (http://www.burkespeerage.com)

Census - CSO - Central Statistics Office (http://www.cso.ie/census)

Chambers, Anne (2003). Ireland's Pirate Queen: The True Story of Grace O'Malley. New York: MJF Books. ISBN 978-1-56731-858-6

Clew Bay Archaeological Trail (http://www.clewbaytours.com)

Clew Bay Heritage Centre (http://www.westportheritage.com)

Cunningham, Deirdre, PhD (2005). Brackloon – The Story of an Irish Oak Wood. (http://www.coford.ie)

Discover Ireland (http://www.discoverireland.com)

Enhanced British Parliamentary Papers on Ireland (http://www.dippam.ac.uk/eppi)

Knox: The History of County Mayo (http://www.askaboutireland.ie/reading-room/digital-book-collection/digital-books-by-county/mayo/knox-the-history-of-the-c/)

InfoMar – Clew Bay (http://www.infomar.ie/surveying/Bays/Clewv1.php)

Ireland Grid Reference (http://www.gridreference.ie)

Irish Birding (http://www.irishbirding.com)

Irish Wrecks (http://www.irishwrecks.com)

National Archives: Census of Ireland (http://www.census.nationalarchives.ie)

Ordnance Survey Ireland (http://www.osi.ie)

The Reek (http://www.thereek.com)

Tóchar Phádraig (http://www.ballintubberabbey.ie/tochar-phadraic)

Index

Index

Index

Index

About the author

Michael Cusack first climbed Croagh Patrick at the age of six and has since enjoyed over one hundred ascents of the mountain. He has led multi-week cycling and hiking tours in both Europe and the United States and has lived and worked in several countries, including Saudi Arabia, France, England, Austria, and the United States. His travel experience has included several treks in the Everest and Annapurna regions of Nepal, as well as Mount Kilimanjaro in Tanzania and Kosciuszko, the highest peak in Australia. A former Irish cycling squad member, he raced extensively in Europe and the USA. His family have lived in the Westport area for generations and his grandfather Peter Hopkins was one of the last Clew Bay pilots. Michael is now a guide for Reek Tours in the Westport area (www.thereek.com).

Peter Hopkins, the author's grandfather and one of the last Westport Bay pilots, used to stay on Inishlyre or Island More when the weather prevented him from returning home to Rosbeg. c.1960 (Picture courtesy of Fiona Hopkins)